# LIVING IN THE
# BROKEN WEST
## ESSAYS

MIKE MEDBERRY

For John Freemuth

A family man, ardent conservationist, teacher, runner, friend, and all-around good soul.

*"May your trails be crooked, winding, lonesome, dangerous, leading to the most amazing view. May your mountains rise into and above the clouds.... Where something strange and more beautiful, more full of wonder than your deepest dreams await you—beyond that next turning of the canyon walls."*

Edward Abbey

Text:
©2022 by Mike Medberry

Photographs:
Unless credited otherwise, ©2022 by Mike Medberry


Mike Medberry, *author*

Colleen Brennan, Lisa Theobald, *editors*

Toni Rome, guyrome.com, *graphic designer*


About the Cover:
"The Wolf Watches." Will Caldwell's painting of a wolf nervously watching a classic old car speeding down the highway outside of Ketchum, Idaho.


ISBN 979-8-9854316-1-2 Kindle ebook

ISBN 979-8-9854316-0-5 print

Library of Congress number: 2021925156

Essay subjects: 1. Health and sickness, stroke; 2. The Los Angeles River rehabilitation; running; 3. finding home; Gila Monster; 4. War and Wilderness;  5. The Bears Ears, Arch Canyon; 6. French Creek, primitive areas; 7. Arctic; National Petroleum Reserve in Alaska; Inupiat; 8. Boise River, Sawtooth Wilderness; 9. Living well


Medberry, Michael Chauncey, 1956; Living in the Broken West: Essays

**FISH HAWK PUBLISHING**

P.O. BOX 140845, GARDEN CITY, ID 83714

# CONTENTS

# INTRODUCTION

Why, you might ask, is the West broken?

The lead essay, "On the Dark Side of the Moon," is my story about having a severe stroke in Craters of the Moon National Monument and Preserve. It was a horrendous event in my life that changed my perspective on who I was. I was broken, damaged goods, and no damned good to anyone for a couple of years. But, as one character in a Monty Python film says, "Aye gaht bettah." But recovery was much slower than I had thought, much more painful than I had imagined: piece-by-piece persevering through new impediments one-by-one. Ernest Hemingway wrote in *A Farewell to Arms*, "The world breaks everyone and afterward many are strong at the broken places. But those that will not break it kills." It's nice to feel my broken places. This essay is a cautionary tale on brokenness, a metaphor for the need to seize the day in a land that appears broken.

The essay on the L.A. River is a tale of wanton destruction and remarkable recovery. Maybe it is a tale of changing visions. The L.A. River was built as a mostly concrete waterway after floods destroyed part of Los Angeles in the 1930s, '40s, and '50s. It was the home of my father, and L.A. still holds a grand piece of my heart. This is my favorite essay because I learned what may have happened to my father, who died young of brain cancer and a stroke. That walk was a journey of discovery—it had a few moments of terror and some of joy—the kinds of moments that give one the adrenaline to continue walking … or to flat-out run. But I found the L.A. a new river through the city of Los Angeles that I had never seen before. The Friends of the L.A. River have done the hard work of bringing that river back to respectfulness. It was broken, and remains so, but it is as lovely to me as the Grand Canyon of the Colorado River. And it is every bit as dangerous.

"Violence on a Run" is a short vignette of a run that I took in Santa Fe on a hot day. It was deeply bothering to me because a woman was running from a violent man and I somehow found myself in the midst of the man's anger. And then that threat just disappeared. I ran away. That haunted me. What had happened? How was it resolved? Did she come back to that brutal partner of hers? You talk about broken… There are a number of essays that are very short and resolve little—for example, "Meditation on the Death of Two Women," "Home," and "A Fool's Drunken Pilgrimage in Search of a Gila Monster," but they seem to me to illustrate singular ideas that cannot be made otherwise.

"French Creek," "Hiking on the Solstice," and "Walking Up the Boise River" are about some of my favorite places. And I'll tell you, the Boise River is one messed-up and broken place, but it does serve many of our needs. All three of these essays describe places that are delightful but dangerous. "Sacred Dirt" was written after more than 30 years and many trips hiking in Arch Canyon and thinking about its past and likely future—it provides less of the environmental groups' message but is nuanced with all of those years of consideration and intense observation.

I want to mention the iconic cover of my book: Will Caldwell's painting of a wolf standing, leering, at a road outside Ketchum watching a very classy car driving quickly below, headed, I imagine, to Redfish Lake to the Wild Idaho conference. The painting speaks to me of the uncertainty that wolves living in Idaho face: guns, traps, poison, snares, helicopter hunting, foul attitudes, and whatever else you can think of. The Idaho Legislature favors cows and sheep over wolves and bison and has a collective fear of wild things. Some of Idaho's legislators have the hubris to try to reduce the recovery of wolves to the very minimum. They have that power. But wolves have long been supported by the vast majority of Idahoans. Recently, the legislature has asserted its primacy over mere citizens in more ways that I choose to innumerate. However, the cover is a statement of hope for wolves and, frankly, for all of life that we seem to be trampling. Things of the heart, equivocal wolves in our hearts. Imagine what you might be looking for as that wolf. I wrote an essay about wolf recovery but chose not to include it in this collection, as it was filled with vitriol and damnation of churlish politicians; it didn't seem to embrace hope.

That's the thing about this collection, it is about hope, a skittish hope. A distant hope for humankind that is stated best in the last, short, short essay, "Football Playing in Boise."

I hope you enjoy reading all of the essays in this collection, some of which I have not described in this introduction (e.g., the longest, "Flight," which is about my mother's life), but if you don't, please write me a scurrilous note. I would like that. Honestly, I would. But be forewarned, I'm a cranky old cuss, as cranky as the survivor of an unearned stroke can be, and I may respond in kind. Better, however, I would like to hear how we might, together, reform this broken West and make it into a singular place that will be as good as the one we've ruthlessly stolen from wolves and bison.

*Mike Medberry*

# DARK SIDE OF THE MOON

G iven half a thought, I might have remembered that taking a stroll in the Craters of the Moon National Monument in Idaho is like walking on the dark side of the moon. It's true that the peaceful, oil-painting look of the desert and the contrast of black lava with the clear, cobalt sky are stunning. But this is a lonely place, an alien, rugged, deserted, fabulous, and dangerous place. It is a jaunt through a landscape of *a'a* lava, a place of broken and sooty saucers and teacups, for miles and miles and miles. To be exact, Craters is 54 miles north to south and 25 from east to west. In addition, this vast area supports no flowing rivers or creeks. It is hot desert for most of the year, the lava regularly reaching temperatures of 140 degrees Fahrenheit, and it is a subzero desert during the dead of winter. What I can tell you certainly is that Craters of the Moon is a hell of a place to lie stranded and facing death. But I get ahead of myself.

This land of volcanic debris is on a remote road between Carey and Arco, both tiny ranching towns in Eastern Idaho, on the edge of the enormous, evil-seeming Idaho National Laboratory nuclear research and testing center, which no one can legally enter without an invitation. And don't count on being invited here, because this enormous piece of land is contaminated by nuclear waste in places—something that almost no one speaks of. This is an eerie location, to be sure, but you don't have to be invited to go to the adjacent Craters of the Moon National Monument. Walking into its depths takes you into a seldom visited place. It can be a painful walk that burns and bruises your feet, twists your ankles, and makes topsy-turvy your sense of balance. There are few trails through the lava, and those who walk here risk the rubber of their boot soles being torn up by the sharp rocks and ridges of lava that run like serrated knives across the landscape. It is best to prepare for all conditions before you go to Craters of the Moon.

What the hell was I doing here on this April day? I'm an environmentalist; that is my only excuse. Four of us—Miguel, Katie, Doug, and I—planned to meet Secretary of Interior Bruce Babbitt because he had recommended that Craters of the Moon National Monument be expanded from 54,000 acres to more than 750,000 acres.

*Pictured Left: Hiking out of darkness.*
PHOTO: DOUG SCHNITZSPAHN

We wanted to convey some information—especially about how little grazing was being done in Laidlaw Park—to Babbitt. We drove four hours from Boise to spend a couple of days camping and hiking

*Dwarf monkeyflowers give hope.*

here. We came to gain on-the-ground information about issues such as the effects of livestock grazing, hunting, water use, and off-road vehicle use on delicate lava formations. We wanted to check the current conditions of plants such as miniature monkeyflowers and dwarf buckwheat; animals including mule deer, badger, and red fox; and archeological sites. All four of us wanted to say, truthfully, to any critics, "I know that land by foot, not by hearsay or speculation, and here is how it looks...."

I especially wanted to look again at Laidlaw Park, which is a *kipuka*, a Hawaiian word for an island of soil and grass surrounded by lava—in this case, miles of lava from the Great Rift lava flow. At 84,400 acres, the Laidlaw Park kipuka is said to be the largest kipuka in the United States, and it supports many unique plants and animals. This parched but fertile land is remote and lacks water, and it is open only to limited livestock grazing. Therefore, it is not as damaged as most of the overgrazed public lands in the United States.

After we arrived, we walked for an hour over a solid lava flow, where sagebrush grew like whiskers on a roughened face. When we could afford to look up instead of at our feet, we saw an endless reach of pure black rock and dark stretches of volcanic rubble. In April, Craters of the Moon has a Jekyll-and-Hyde persona—cold, sleety squalls storm across the land and wind brings an icy fog, but then the emerging sun will suddenly provide a warm spell for a few minutes. As we hiked, we experienced the full force of this movement between two sides of its personality, and once in a while, the land seemed kissed by a fleeting beam of sunlight.

After another hour of walking through the day's on-and-off inclement weather, we reached Little Laidlaw Park. There, we stopped and looked south into its big brother, Big Laidlaw Park, which provided an oceanic expanse of blowing grasses. The piebald grasslands of the Laidlaw Park kipuka formed a quilt of roughly spun black-and-tan wool. The surrounding lava looked fluid, as even its stony wrinkles indicated movement and grasses flowed in waves. We continued on in the rain and crossed a raised isthmus of lava that offered a sweeping view of the new lands slated to be included in the monument.

As the four of us stood staring at the view, I realized I had a bad headache. When had this killer headache come on? I asked Katie for an aspirin—no, make it two—and then walked away to look out over the endless view. Earlier that day, before we had begun hiking, I had stumbled, oddly, in the campground. That seemed weird, tripping on nothing. Now, as we sat atop Bowl Crater, my headache was excruciating, and aspirin did nothing to abate it as I tried to shake my throbbing head into sense.

This point was the farthest north we had walked, and as we turned back to the south to head to our cars, we were enveloped in a strange, soothing, blowing mist—a cold, distancing mist. I thought how it would feel to get into my Subaru and relax. I thought about a beer, a Moosehead beer, chips with red-hot salsa, and warming my hands by the heater. My friends plodded on with their heads buried in raincoat hoods as we crossed the stormy sea of black rock. There were no trails out here, but we figured we'd meet at the two cars parked at Laidlaw Park if we lost sight of each other.

I hopped through the lava in this barren landscape and my head felt better. But then I stumbled on nothing, and my head smacked with a crack on the lava. I awoke suddenly, feeling incoherent. My legs were useless and my thoughts incongruent and I shook my head to straighten my sensibilities. I had hit my head hard, and I was blank, yet I felt pain—not from the outside, exactly … no, not quite … but from somewhere I couldn't quite touch. I tried to break out of this gauzy consciousness to figure out what had cast me down on the lava and to yell, "Hey, guys, wait up!" to my disappearing friends. But I couldn't sit up to yell.

I looked around to see who or what had taken me down and felt terribly confused. There was nothing particular to see, and I had no clue about what had just happened. My breath shortened as I groaned and rolled over on the hard lava. I could barely move in this new world that was all wrong in time and seemed to have no limits. What had happened? A heart attack, a banged head, a gunshot? It couldn't be any sort of affliction: I was 44 years old and in good condition. I'd run a half-marathon the day before, for God's sake, finished 88th out of 2,200 people. And I was a marathoner, too, having run two Boston Marathons. Yet I lay immobilized on this lava. What was this about? Had I tripped and fallen unconscious? I hadn't heard a shot, and there was no one there who could have fired a gun. But nothing could have been quicker to lay me down, and my mind just seemed short-circuited, regardless of the knot on my head. It might have been a bolt of lightning.

As I lay in this desolate land, my consciousness drifted to a place I'd never been. I felt a blankness, not knowing exactly what had occurred. In and out of consciousness, in and out of pain, in and out of reality, I simply did not know what was real. I felt the intermittent sun and rain and hard mist on my face and smelled the sage. This was real: the smell of sagebrush, the wetness of rain, the hardness of rock, the sun on my body. But in a second I knew I'd be up and walking. Surely, it was just a receding pain, a little quirk, or a pinprick— like forgetting my keys for a moment, or stumbling on a pebble.

But I was slipping away. To my friends, I must've simply disappeared in one of the famous April squalls. The three of them would get back to their cars and wonder about me. They would be annoyed, and then they'd think I had gotten lost. My real predicament was just too improbable to be considered. They'd wait for an hour for me to arrive, then two, then three. Perhaps they'd worry and look for me, but where would they look? Already it was late afternoon, and the town of Carey, the cow town we had driven through on our way to Laidlaw Park, was an hour and a half away. Even if someone found me, what then? I knew I was in trouble beyond what I could fathom.

I couldn't put my feet under me, and I felt as if they were lost somehow—I couldn't even see them. When I tried to signal, no one was there to respond, and what should have been hoots and hollers sounded oddly like grunts and mumbles. I couldn't understand my own garbled words. I couldn't talk, I couldn't yell, I couldn't walk or crawl. I was reduced to the gurgling sounds of a baby and confused beyond belief. I didn't know what I didn't know.

Inert on the lava, I tried to take some sort of inventory of my life. I looked out at the world with one good eye, like the monstrous eye of a Cyclops. Why was the world so bleary in the other? My right eye must have been bloody, because it was wet and hurting. I could feel that, but I couldn't see much of anything from that eye. And I didn't know how long I had lain there—had it been minutes, seconds, hours? I had absolutely no idea, and no one else was there—where had they gone?

I turned over, pushing with my left arm. My face was caked with something, either dirt or blood, or probably both. My right leg wouldn't work, and my right arm was as limp as a shot rabbit. But my left shoulder had life in it. Left arm, same. Left leg, same. Well, then, surely I could move and stand and walk. I agonized and almost managed to push up on my left arm but fell repeatedly. My face felt like it had been hatcheted in two, as blood ran down one side; I could taste its sharp metallic, salty tang, and I could feel the warm liquid on my face. I had fallen hard enough on the rough lava to draw blood. I wiped the blood from my good hand on my blue jeans and on my bright yellow rain jacket.

OK, I thought, I'll get out of this myself. That's what I'd always done before, proudly fixed myself. But now something was going bad with my mind—was it my concentration, or was my life leaking out onto the lava? I felt deadened, until a quick sharpness of pain shot though me. I felt dizzy, couldn't think, moved in slow motion; my mind spun as if caught in a hurricane. Was it hours or minutes when I quit trying to do what was once in my power to do? Running, skipping, walking, crawling, finding the fascinating beauty in this place, and telling the stories I wanted to tell of the spectacular oddness in Craters of the Moon.

The stories, these stories, were what sustained me as a writer, gave me clarity, a sense of humor, a sense of repartee, and the ability to express myself. Now the lava ripped at my skin as I moved, heavy headed as a slow monster, and I felt no humor. I again felt my right

*A look through
a damaged land
toward inspiration.*

leg and arm. I couldn't believe it—nothing. No feeling at all. What
the hell was happening? I felt disembodied, alien, alone, and utterly
frustrated. How did I get myself into this mess?

My mind moved randomly to the past. I remembered when
my 54-year-old father, Ray, had a stroke. I was twelve and couldn't
understand it then, but could he have experienced this same feeling?
My father, who was a lawyer, had been rendered speechless. He
could not communicate a thing in speech. I remember that when he
was in the hospital, he wore a white turban to hide where the doctors
had opened up his head. It was stitched and bandaged, and he wore
a pirate's eyepatch. My father pointed, shook his finger, and grunted
as he looked out the window of Tripler Hospital, a military hospital in
Hawaii. As a 12-year-old, I was baffled by my feeling of helplessness
and his inability to connect with me. But he understood me and I
understood he wanted the hell out of the hospital. Surely that was
what he wanted; he felt trapped inside himself. Six months later my
father was dead. Now I knew a piece of his death, the torture of it
firsthand. I got the picture. Now I needed to get out of this goddamned
trap of black rock. My God, make me whole again!

The lava proved a terrible obstacle. I slid down the slanted piece I was lying on and caught a branch so I wouldn't slide farther. Everything blurred. I held onto the branch with all my strength—if I let go, I feared sliding upside-down into heavier brush, and I would be completely lost from all sight. It seemed so urgent to have my hand on that branch. I felt my unique and mercurial senses: the fear of sliding, the taste of blood, the smell and sensation of the coming and going rain, the sound of my pumping heart, and my fear of dying. I felt afraid of what little I saw in the dark, hot and cold, lonely lava.

I felt thirsty from yesterday's run. I had no water bottle because I had forgotten to pack one in my hurry to leave town. There had been no water at the campground where we camped the night before, and that day on the lava I had no cup to catch the rain when it fell. I knew that having no water could cost me my life in a few hours if I didn't get help. If night came and I stayed out in the elements, what chance would I have? So I held onto the branch for life, because I could feel that one thing clearly. The fragrance of the desert engulfed me: the sweet smells of sagebrush, the rusted odor of iron, bitter rabbitbrush, and the oil-rich smell of the earth.

Somehow, as I passed out and woke up several times, I held onto that branch. Once I awoke to see the sun shining brightly and the clouds sending out spokes of light. Later, clouds darkened half the sky and virga dramatically fell, threatening rain, as the day grew shorter. The sun would soon go down, and I could only think of dying a pathetic death on a mild April night, with a 40-degree temperature slowly draining my body's heat. My heartbeats measured the day, which held no time, only heartbeats and breaths. I felt a pain in my chest and called out to the earth, but what use was that? What good was this silent earth that I'd worked 20 years to protect? Now I was rooted in among simple rocks and bushes. I tried to move, but with only one leg and one hand, I moved in circles. I closed my eyes, breathed heavily, listened to my heart beat, and tried to think about my circumstances. I cried for mercy to no one and everyone, and I cried for love. Crying was not usually something I did, but I was crying now. My life as I had known it for 44 years was disappearing in a blink. In a blink of time, I was nothing that I recognized as me.

The rain from a minute-long outburst chilled me to the bone. The rough *a'a* lava had become both my friend and my worst enemy: in the sunlight, it cooked me, and when the rain came, I shivered. The water that collected in little depressions of the *a'a* evaporated in minutes, and I couldn't get a drink. Life was elemental on this lava. When a spider walked by my good eye, I tried to move away, but it kept on coming until I screamed inarticulately and blew it away from me. How could I survive if I could barely divert the path of a spider? I waited. I had no choice.

My thoughts shifted intermittently between an awareness of my body and an awareness of what I needed to do. That struck me as funny, "what I needed to do." I wasn't going anywhere at all and the sun was going down. My hopes for saving more of this piece of land might be lost if I couldn't get my ass up and get going quickly. I saw the sun in bright, psychedelic, exaggerated colors of orange, red, and clear yellow, and I hung onto the branch when I couldn't so much as see it. I could *feel* it. This was something of this world I could focus on. My consciousness was constantly slipping away since I had fallen, and my head felt weighted by a ton of lead. My physical and psychological incompetence grew.

I wanted to move in a sensible, straight direction but I couldn't do it. I had to get up, but after unknowable hours of trying, I had to concede I couldn't fight it. Fighting was entirely futile. I lived inside of death, looking out at a dark animal that stood with his heavy paws on me, keeping me immobile. I was beaten in a decisive manner I couldn't even have imagined a few hours ago. I closed my eyes and tried to make this horrible mirage disappear, but my mind whispered that it had come to me for a reason, that I should just enjoy the life that was still here. I might as well watch this world going on, going away, and going out.

I became a pure observer for the first time in my life, watching the land with my one seeing eye. I breathed heavily and deeply in the chill air and knew that this day would surely outlive me. I'd be flesh and bones, still and dead, by tomorrow's morning. I felt myself a part of this burned-out landscape, no more than the lava and no less. I gave myself to it, to its warmth, to its brightness, to its burning rays, to its cold stillness. It was uncanny to feel entirely at peace in this way; I have never felt such calmness and quietness, and I suppose I never will again. What would happen next simply would, because I had no power to change anything. I could only watch and feel my life in exquisite detail, with smells of life and the light of day as they began to merge and disappear. It became a time of pure calm, an unparalleled peace and balance, and somehow I felt in harmony with life and this land. Dying would not be so terrible at all; it beckoned like a smooth slip down a slide into warm water.

I don't know how long I lay there, but I saw a vision as one of my friends emerged from the mist. In a flash I again wanted life. In a moment, the desire for peace in dying turned into the turmoil and bustle of living. I called, "Kah-to! Ree-ta!" I could suddenly reach Doug in this unlimited lava. He heard me. "Kf-tah!" I've got his attention. He's turning this way. "Fu-fat!" Thank God! He's here! I'm saved! There would be no peace in my dying now.

Doug walked toward me and then stopped short. He was horrified at my condition, he told me much later. He called for Katie and Miguel. Most of the blood on my face had dried, and one side drooped like the jowls of a basset hound. I had been there four or more hours while they searched for me. They searched in a line, side-by-side, in the rugged lava, and planned to give it up in half an hour, when darkness would fall. Only by luck had daylight held out in this ruby sunset.

My body hung like an awkward question mark, my good arm hugging the branch with all the strength I had. Doug could see I had fallen oddly and didn't want to move me. My right arm and leg were both awry, and Doug thought I had a broken neck. The three of them decided to move me very carefully to a level and grassier place. Then Katie went off in a hurry for help. She must have taken two or three hours to cross the kipuka to reach her car, drive into town to make a phone call, and then return with a group of rescuers. When I talked with her afterward, she said she was frantic. At one point, she took a wrong turn. She'd gone 35 miles in the wrong direction, and she was almost out of gas. But she made it back.

My leg wasn't useable as I lay on the lava, and Doug took my shoes from me for a reason I'll never understand. I wanted my shoes, was indignant about their loss. Later he told me that by taking my shoes, he thought he could keep me from trying to walk. As if I could! And I desperately wanted water. But Doug looked at me and fell silent, believing that water was the wrong thing to give me. He walked away to smoke a cigarette and collect his thoughts. I recall his smoking vividly, because Doug was no smoker. I think he got one from Miguel. Miguel gave me a cup of yogurt, which I opened with one hand and spilled all over myself. It was subsistence. I wanted to walk away but, of course, I couldn't. I passed out, came back, and hummed to stay awake at Doug's insistence. I hummed with Miguel's songs and held on because I knew I was being saved.

After Katie finally returned, a helicopter landed like a big dragonfly in a nearby grassy area. Several men moved slowly on the lava with their flashlights, like fireflies. One man put a scarf over my face as if I were dead, and three or four men put me onto a stretcher, lifting, grunting, and stumbling as they carried me to the helicopter and slid me into it. They were all the ghosts of magic, gliding across the kipuka and rough lava to save my life. I rose in the helicopter and was flown to a hospital about 45 miles in a line across Idaho's Great Rift, south, to Pocatello. It had been six hours since I had fallen on the lava.

In the act of attempting to protect Idaho's natural landscape, I had broken myself, and now I would have to rehabilitate my body as well as trying to rehabilitate this land I loved. I was facing a long fight to bring back any sense of coherence and quality in my life. Regaining 20 years of building my profession, my loves, my thinking, my speech, my writing, and all of the work protecting Craters of the Moon, everything of my life that really mattered seemed erased. What was left of me? I couldn't know the magnitude of the struggle before me or the energy it would take to bring myself back from this deadly injury. The task of protecting Craters of the Moon faded from my priorities. This is where that stormy April day had deposited me, and I wouldn't forget that. Unraveling this confusion—relearning to walk, to speak, to advocate for conservation, to write, to count, to cook, to work, to live, and to love—would take geologic time.

*Daisies growing on lava.*

# WALKING THE
# L.A. RIVER

*Maybe there is a place where I could talk over this river with you, to grieve for this poor, damned stretch of water that has been concreted and cursed, routed and rerouted, pumped, poisoned, peopled, and picked at like a war victim. We could speak of rocket testing and the nuclear meltdown that happened in 1955. We might touch on the Los Angeles River being a race strip for fast cars in sexy films. But let's not; let's speak triumphantly of the river's future, to talk about what I have found, maybe connive to fix some of its serious problems and have it solve yours and mine, to come close to this river for solace and exercise. Or maybe we could find a coyote or cougar living in and passing through the river corridor like some shadow. This river is home to many, simply a place with undoubted and evanescent value. But the L.A. River, as they say, weaves a more complicated story, and it begins like this:*

The Los Angeles River originates in the Santa Susana and San Gabriel Mountains in Los Angeles County. It flows into the San Fernando Valley through Los Angeles and Pasadena, emptying into the Pacific Ocean at the port of Long Beach. It runs smack-dab through the city of Los Angeles, beside anonymous industrial buildings and railroad tracks, under overpasses, and over sacred land. It issues less than a hiss on most days when it is overwhelmed by the roaring city traffic. On uncertain other days, however, it howls, wrapping around bridge pylons and carrying houses on its back, muddy water rising like a tidal wave.

The L.A. River was once an ephemeral stream, growing with spring rains, but otherwise mostly a dry gulch. Swamps and lakes that existed in the early years of the 20th century dried up on the river's coastal plain because of groundwater pumping for agricultural and residential uses. Ephemeral streams are notoriously sneaky: they flash-flood or sleep, flowing in a torrent or a trickle, and it was just these conditions that led to the modern incarnation of the river. The floods of 1933 and 1938 came as unexpected disasters. In 1933, 400 homes washed away. In 1938, 115 people died, and 5,600 homes were destroyed. Major storms occurred

*Pictured Left: The L.A. River flowing through the city below the San Gabriel Mountains.*

in 1815, 1825, 1861, 1914, 1969, and 2005, but the floods occurring after 1960 were less damaging because of flood control projects.

People who owned valuable buildings along this slow, meandering river were surprised in the 1930s to see the water rising above their eyeballs and raging down the watercourse, ripping along with it lives, homes, possessions, and fragile hopes. Naturally they were angry and blamed the confounded river rather than themselves—no one chooses to accept blame for building too close to a river. The U.S. Army Corps of Engineers, with growing fame for its feats of controlling nature through flood control dams, answered the calls for help in 1934 and 1938 and throughout the '40s. The L.A. River became just an anonymous series of concrete ditches as the work of the Army Corps of Engineers and hundreds of volunteers proceeded. The river, once slithering like a rattlesnake through town, now lay defanged by the Corps and a motivated contingency of the public. We lost the namesake river to a city of traffic jams.

### Now is the time for the L.A. River

While visiting Los Angeles, I talked with longtime architect Bill Coburn as he remembered the L.A. floods of 1938, at age 11. He is a sharp man, and I could sense his joy and love of nature. "In the '30s we went right down by the river here behind us and there were sand dabs, frogs, and birds. It was a very nice place." Coburn beamed with the memory. "In 1938 we got eight or ten inches of rain, and the water got behind the concrete that was put into the channel after the earlier flood, and it ripped and tore the concrete to pieces." Bill's father's design firm had planned much of the repair work. "It was all very vulnerable and every little street had a bridge and every bridge was swept away by the water. There were even alligators loose in Lincoln Park Lake!"

Bill laughed at the thought of alligators in downtown L.A. and told a story about riding his bike through a raging river to deliver newspapers. He got caught on a cable in the current, and by some kind of good fortune, he was able to leave his bike there as he finished the paper route. He said that was the last time he tried to fight the river. "Now, after the Corps controlled the river, it is coming back and has been restored. There are kayaks and canoes and ducks and geese in the Sepulveda flood basin. There are fish in the river again, and it's lovely!"

Today the L.A. River is the most thoroughly urbanized and channelized large stream in the nation. This distinction is epitomized by its being jailed in an engineered-to-perfection concrete ditch channel for 40 miles of its 51-mile length. One-foot-thick reinforced concrete, roughly 400 feet wide and spanning 40 miles, is a stunning engineering feat, and the 3 million barrels of concrete used in construction is roughly the linear equivalent of the concrete poured for the Hoover Dam.

The unsuppressed growth of Los Angeles has had a profound effect on the river. Today it appears to citizens only in occasional glances from the freeway, tucked behind fences, as if it were a prisoner, shamed, criminalized, and pitied, relegated to a trickle in an expansive ditch of sterile concrete. But the river has always been there, working out a plan to escape. It is said that there is a time for everything. Now is the time for the L.A. River.

Come on in!

### Hey, do you know where the L.A. River is?

I have lived much of my life beside wild rivers and untrampled landscapes in the Western outback of Idaho. The L.A. River has terrified me far more than Idaho's Salmon—"the River of No Return"—or the Selway or Colorado Rivers. The only thing to fear in those wild places is nature. But nature is no longer a force along the L.A. River, which has been wounded by men of science and remade to protect human lives from the occasional Noachian floods. Herein lies the problem: We have not remade the L.A. River well. It is straightjacketed, the subject of laughter and pity. We've wiped out much of the river's original wildlife and 95 percent of riparian areas. The floods were a problem well solved by the linear thinking of engineers in our multitasking world.

When I was growing up in L.A. in the 1970s, I lost track of the L.A. River just like almost everyone else had; it lay so harmless, so emasculated, and so mostly hidden from sight. Now, more than 40 years later, I returned to look at what the L.A. River had become and what I thought it might become. I was curious about this switchblade river that I hadn't seen since I was a child. I researched its past, walked for three days along its "banks," traveling from Long Beach to the headwaters in the Santa Susana Mountains. I spoke with advocates for rehabilitating the river and tried to talk to the Army Corps of Engineers about the agency's dreams and work in the basin.

*Palms grace Elysian Park.*

I flew into L.A. in March and found a motel somewhere in the middle of the ancient river plain and planned to walk the river. The next day I rented a camping van and drove and drove and drove, but by the time I got off the 405, the 105, the 110, and Interstate 5, I might have been almost anywhere. There was no river that I could see when I stopped at L.A.'s large and heavily used Griffith Park, with its many paths, many palm and sycamore trees, and much traffic. I parked my van in a safe place with other cars and began walking on an old road. There was beauty in this part of the park as I climbed down and up a big, rocky hill across the road to find the river. (Where else would you look for a lost river but from the highest hill?) I stood on Angels Point, which overlooks the massive city of Los Angeles and Dodger Stadium, with the Dodgers inside running, hitting, sliding, and catching the ball in Chavez Ravine, like all dodgers should do; the booming voice of the announcer revealed the score amidst a vast parking lot that, once upon a time, was a rural village on the banks of a small river.

I saw a piece of the L.A. River far, far away down below, and sweet, young hoodlums standing before me, talkin' trash and drinkin' Tuborg beer. The clean air shocked me—it was clean! I had never experienced clean air in L.A. when I grew up in the city. And the beer they shared refreshed. There, at last, was the river that I had come to see. We talked about it and I heard wonder in their voices. These were my natural friends, the lovers of a river.

Forty years ago, L.A. was lousy with stinky, snaky, brown, ubiquitous smog; it stole my breath and held an acrid ozone-and-coal smell that made me lazy. I hated L.A. for the smog and was glad to leave this mess of a city for Sacramento. As I stood on that hill, the air was as sweet and pure as the blooming jacaranda trees. Such was the consequence of passing time and the incremental, growing civic concern about human health. This place pleased me enormously, and I was again surprised when an owl hooted in the eucalyptus trees amidst the thrum of traffic and police whistles.

In 1930, the famed architecture firms Olmstead Brothers and Bartholomew Associates proposed a visionary plan for the city of Los Angeles, with greenways connecting parks and running along the river. However, real estate developers and the city council quickly buried it. The plan would have come at the price of managing the river, providing playgrounds in many places and preserving the valuable Southern California beaches as undeveloped parks. It was more brilliant than real estate developers could stand, and they held the checkbook. Today, however, the Olmstead plan stands for what L.A. might have been and could be once again. For 80 years, the city has grown and its possibilities have radically changed, but the plan remains an iconic blueprint for the city to this day.

### Finding safety: a goose in the railyard

The next morning, I parked my car at the L.A. River Garden Park, took a hectic metro train through the city down to Long Beach, and began hiking the first 20 miles from the Pacific Ocean to the railyards, just below downtown L.A. I began at the outlet of the river to the sea, an odd-seeming place, where the RMS *Queen Mary* is permanently docked in the harbor as a symbol of something like hope. People wandered in the park beside the river's mouth. The place where the river widened and mixed with the ocean formed a rich estuary for many kinds of wildlife.

The long and hot bike path was easy to follow as I walked upriver through impoverished neighborhoods. There is little to tell about the first several miles, except that I endured it and saw many citizen-based efforts to improve the river along the way. Several sub-watershed and recreation plans on this lower stretch of the river aim to restore the badly damaged ecosystems in L.A. Along the river path, bicycle riders are surprisingly numerous, which made me feel a growing appreciation for this place. Pelicans, cormorants, gulls, vultures, coots, and mallard ducks flew above and kept miserable company with me in the desiccating heat of day. I saw men camped on the riverbank, surviving on next to nothing, along with ubiquitous shopping carts and souped-up bicycles that lay around. Occasionally, I stopped to eat or explore under one of the more than 100 bridges along the route.

Many miles upriver, when I thought my day's hiking was near its end, I found myself locked out of the river corridor by vertical concrete river walls built by the Corps of Engineers. It reminded me of the Parunuweap fork of the Virgin River, a canyon in Southern Utah, where vertical rock forces you to swim or climb above the creek. I really didn't want to walk in the green ooze of this river, because I had already slipped on the incredibly slick river-on-concrete and had slimed my knees. So I left the river and reenergized myself with a Coke and some nice, greasy GMO yam fries.

I called Chauncey IV, my cousin who lives in L.A. (and the son of Chauncey Joseph Medberry III, who had been a teller in the Bank of Italy and then its president and chairman of the board after it became the Bank of America), to tell him where I was. I was in Vernon, a small town set amidst industrial buildings. He told me not to go walking in that dangerous area and not to go down to the river. He suggested taking a cab. Oh well, I said, it was only a little ways back to my car. I didn't tell him that none of the maps that I carried would be helpful for navigating or that my magical cell phone was on the blink and soon would be out of power. I'll be careful, I told him, and re-entered the canyon of this wounded river. It wasn't at all like the Virgin River in Utah, but the current still flowed downhill.

I scoured several blocks for access to the concrete canal and finally found a side canyon. I passed several tents and the gathered utensils and implements of their residents, people I came to think of as being much like the indigenous Tongva and Gabrieleno people. I climbed through a cut in the fence to the river path. I had read that the Gabrieleno and Tongva were killed off or held as laborers by the Spanish, Mexican missionaries, and later by the Yanks. They were the native Californians when the Spanish arrived in 1769 with their weapons and firewater. Before that, Native Americans had lived peacefully in the sun, in this land of milk and honey, drinking from the river and eating steelhead, lamprey, acorns, deer, squirrels, and other game that no longer exists in L.A. They lived close to the land and learned to respect the rhythms of the storms in this near-desert climate. For that, they were enslaved and killed or taught other ways to live.

In 2016, riverside campers seemed to be living a tribal life, living on the banks of the river, hiding out under the protection of bridges, foraging on city streets and bringing salvaged food to their camps. These nouveau Native Americans had bicycles, skateboards, and other valuable modes of transportation. (After all, this *is* L.A.) They were living in the solitude of a canyon, surrounded by millions and millions of upside people. I tiptoed beside these camps and hoped that the inhabitants were not at home, because I did not feel safe here. No one came out to greet me, and I assumed that they were out for a long day seeking contributions from the public or somewhere out drinking firewater. They were making a living, but not one that I would want. I moved on quickly, feeling rich, conspicuous, and vulnerable.

When twilight came, I had an uncertain number of miles before I would get back to my van. I saw beautiful bridges that Bureau of Reclamation planners had designed to span the river during the years of 1910 to the late 1930s. Their designs were intricate and artful and at least one of them, the Sixth Street Bridge, has been redesigned to glorify L.A. and its river.

*Graffiti announces the Frog Pond.*

Upon one wall above the river I found many intricate murals in a graffiti code that I didn't understand. I photographed some of the illustrations. Beside the wall, brush grew profusely and, as it turned out, provided homes for wandering people. Two of them popped up and one walked along the wall with a spray can. I hid my camera and waved to them. The camera is worth a fortune to me, and it would provide a fortune to those who have nothing, so I stuffed it in my pack and walked on into the coming darkness.

*The Fourth St. viaduct bridge was built in 1928 across the L.A. River. This and other bridges crossing the river near downtown were inspired by civic architecture from Paris and Rome.*

A bit farther upstream, I stopped and took pictures of one of the most striking bridges I had seen. When I looked back at the men, they were looking my way, holding steady at a distance. They began nonchalantly following me. What I had done was clear enough to me. I stuffed the camera back into my pack and took off running. I looked back as one of my apparent pursuers ducked down. Looked again and another ducked. I took off again and didn't stop running until I glided into the railyard above, scanning a long series of coupled trains on three or four sets of rails, considering my next move. I didn't know what was inside the open boxcars so I continued jogging quietly beside them and felt certain, almost certain, that no one had seen me. Then I heard the rumbling sound of a freight train and saw its brilliant maniacal headlight coming toward me. I ran faster, fearing—I don't know what. Was it the infamous "bulls" who worked for the company and beat up strangers or the strangers who might be chasing me? Regardless, I didn't plan to find out if there was trouble lurking and ran farther along the train tracks.

Trains rested above the lower canyon of the concrete river and were now isolated from it by a tall fence. I realized that I was trapped between the train tracks and the river, and my heart pounded like a timpani. This seemed the kind of moment where one should turn, look up to the sky, and pray. Instead, I looked down the tracks for a break in the fence and ran some more. I eventually found a hole in the fence. Clearly someone had run this path before me and found a way out. Perhaps this was the route of escape for the Tongva, once upon a time, long, long, long ago. I looked over the wall, found the cement descent moderately safe despite the severely sloping canyon wall, and leapt over before the lights of the train lit my path. I felt safe again in the hardened, barren river drainage below the railyard, which I later found out was called the Piggyback Yard. I felt safer when I found a goose, or she found me, viciously squawking in defense of the five eggs the size of pool balls safe in her nest on the ground.

Safety, I realized, was momentary, fleeting, a contingency dependent upon immediate circumstances. Those eggs would hardly last forever and the goose might learn a tough lesson. I continued searching for a way out and found another cut fence in a dark place under a bridge beside a lonely road. And then I was out and free, walking in this relentless city once again. Soon I found my van among the dark streets and fell into a weary sleep in this damn fine van with the curtains drawn and doors hard-locked.

## The river is an idea

The L.A. River is expected to be partially restored to some of its former glory with help from a most unexpected ally: the U.S. Army Corps of Engineers. The Corps identified 11 miles of river to restore, from Griffith Park, just south of Burbank, to downtown L.A., according to a federal and city of Los Angeles plan. The reason that the Corps defined those 11 miles out of the 51-mile-long river is that this portion of the river has the greatest potential for recovery. The Corps cited the following rationale for restoring this section: (1) The bottom of the river is natural rather than concrete; (2) these 11 miles are surrounded by parkland, including the 4,210-acre Griffith Park and 575-acre Elysian Park; (3) it is connected to promising tributaries, primarily Arroyo Seco, Verdugo Wash, and Tujunga Wash, which will be critical for increasing the biological diversity of the region; and (4) this stretch had strong support for restoration from the city of Los Angeles, the state of California, then Governor Jerry Brown, and many environmental and local citizen advocacy organizations.

The city of Los Angeles supported the broadest alternative (Alt 20) among the Army Corps' proposals for rehabilitating the L.A. River, which would cost $1.08 billion as opposed to the Corps' tentatively selected plan (Alt 13), with a projected cost of $804 million. L.A. Mayor Eric Garcetti told the *L.A. Times* that the city would give an additional $44 million to the Corps' smaller alternative to support restoring the Verdugo Wash, a critical tributary to the L.A. River, and Piggyback Yard. Verdugo Wash is currently fully clad in concrete and would be opened up, while Piggyback Yard would be turned into a marshy riparian area within the city. This was a visionary plan that was nearly inconceivable to me.

One main reason that the restoration plan was finally proposed goes back to the work of the late poet Lewis MacAdams, who in 1986 formed FoLAR, the Friends of the Los Angeles River. FoLAR grew like wildfire. It seemed that MacAdams wasn't alone in his longing for a return to a riverine Los Angeles; many other organizations have grown up alongside FoLAR to restore the river. FoLAR's current goal is to provide a swimmable, fishable, and boatable river. The 5,000-member organization advocates for people using the river and for the birds, fish, mammals, and other life that depend on the river for sustenance.

MacAdams (who died in April 2020) and I talked a few times while I was in L.A., and I interviewed him by phone after I walked up the river. "The L.A. River is raw, not refined in any sense," he said. It's raw and bruised black-and-blue, yet the L.A. River retains its persona. MacAdams once stood, literally, in the way of bulldozers in the river channel. "Desperation is what I felt at the beginning, and I was just working from the seat of my pants," he said. "The river is an idea, an impression confronting what people have done to it." And he felt compassion for it.

The Corps, which created the modern-day L.A. River, has viewed its baby a little differently over the years. But things change and in the environmental review, which the agency prepared, the terms "biodiversity," "connectivity," and "habitat corridors" are used lovingly and have come to have real meaning. I called and visited the Corps office and tried to talk with a spokesman for the Corps in L.A., a nice guy named Jay Field, who wrote that I should try back later after the final decision is made. The Corps of Engineers couldn't tell me how its views have changed to support the restoration of the river, but then it's not exactly in their mandate to be open.

## A cougar runs through it

My feet held 50-cent-sized blisters from the first day of walking up the river from Long Beach to the Los Angeles River Center near where my van was parked. Mostly I had walked on the asphalt bike trail in oppressive SoCal sunshine, along the

*On and on and on, the river runs, through tough and sweet and electrifying places in L.A.*

railroad tracks, and in the river itself. The second day was decidedly different, as I walked upstream from the confluence of Arroyo Seco, beside the Golden State Freeway, and across the river from Elysian Park. I began by crossing the river on the Riverside-Figueroa Bridge, which was in the midst of reconstruction. It was a Sunday and there were no workers on the bridge, so I trespassed and made my way across the bridge without any traffic. Then I walked along the L.A. River Greenbelt, which was very pretty with many trees and golden poppies. But, still, it was an awfully damned long walk.

For the first time in my experience, much of the river actually looked like a river. The flow moved between vegetated islands and along the river's banks—it wasn't the classic, sinuous path of the free-flowing, meandering river that I know in Idaho, but it was a river of some kind. It moved within its hardened walls, rubbing on each side, grumbling and wanting out, it seemed, with ribbons of garbage hanging from tree branches. It was unlike the river downstream, which ran quickly and submissively down the concrete channel of the canal. Herons, egrets, red-tailed hawks, hummingbirds, and other animals were plentiful in this stretch of river. People enjoyed the parks as they fished in the river and fooled around beside the river's living portion. That is the phenomenal quality of a desert river—give a stretch of gravel a little water and life will arise.

The river ran clear in this segment and the flow seemed adequate to sustain life. Smells were pleasant (well, most of them...) and the vegetation lush. I noticed that the temperature of the water in this more natural stream was far cooler than the water running in the concrete channel above or below. There were plenty of dead trees in the flood path to assure that there would be holding water for wildlife and that the river would dilly-dally rather than race directly toward the ocean. There were more butterflies and birds, turtles and squirrels in this section, and a gentleness to the parks built beside the river. The river retains its natural bottom here, including rocks, gravel, and sediment, which are the most honest and fundamental possessions of a living river. People recreated and the breeze cooled as the water laughed by.

One man and I pulled up a big, awkward gate that had come down the river in a flood. He grinned at this catch, his wife shook her head, and I high-fived him and walked on. I thought, "one fewer gate to keep people out." This stretch includes the 11 miles of the natural river bottom that 75 years ago, the Corps claimed had too shallow a water table to risk holding concrete.

That calculation led directly to this almost familiar river experience along the Glendale Narrows, the very section of river slated for restoration, complete with side drainages and new "pocket parks." Most of the homes that back the river here were open, free of iron prison bars and high barbed wire common in other areas along the river. A few of the homes boasted decks with tables and chairs looking conversationally toward the river. The place appeared nicely groomed, safe, and alive.

The rest of the route ran along the near-wilderness of Griffith Park, the place where an oft-photographed cougar lives, endangered by the park's smallness and the roads surrounding it. The cougar's mere presence, however, is testimony to the power of reclaiming lost land. There is no better example of growing wildness in North America than the presence of a cougar here, in the middle of L.A.— and cougars are wily, untamed, usually compassionate to man, but occasionally deadly. This one is in trouble, having been exposed on film to the world by *National Geographic* magazine. Griffith Park looked like an undevelopable place, which could work on the cougar's behalf, but it was surrounded by a punishing city. Can the people of L.A. endure this cougar in their midst? Will they even endure this worthless river? For some reason, they do, so far. Perhaps it is a need expressed by the people of L.A. for wild space and untamed things. They've got all of this in the L.A. River basin.

I walked on the east side of the river, having crossed to maintain a navigable route. I left the corridor just shy of Toluca Lake, where the horse path leads through the elegant L.A. Equestrian Center near the Warner Bros. studio and Forest Lawn cemetery. The vertical walls of the river soon made the route uninteresting and difficult to negotiate, as property lines ran right to the edge of the river wall. There I left the river for a time, grateful for the excuse, but painfully aware that the movie studio and golf course were on private property, property held by a class of people who choose to ignore the river. What have they done to return a portion of their immense profits to restore the river? Not a lot, so far. Some have used it as the steely background for noir films, as a dragstrip for racing cars. Murders occur here and oddly named drugs are sold, but most have never seen the ditch as a living river. It's an odd thing, but can you blame them for wanting to exclude a sight that brings pain?

*A freeway car finds its place to rest, until the next flood.*

## A gathering place for people

I drove to the Sepulveda Basin on Monday morning to begin my third and last day of hiking up the river. The Sepulveda Dam was built in 1941 to catch floodwaters that would otherwise inundate parts of L.A. during flash floods. Sepulveda Basin is a 2,000-acre piece of open land that stands behind this dam and can be opened to release floodwaters when deemed safe. It is a refuge for wildlife and recreationists, as well as the mechanism for flood control. The L.A. River runs through it: the basin is an anomaly in Los Angeles, a truly multiple-use landscape, managed by the Corps and the city of Los Angeles for the use and protection of the city's residents and wildlife. Birds were everywhere, and I thought of Bill Coburn as I walked here.

He was right to be so positive about this flood-catching basin that his firm had designed.

Then I came to the Donald C. Tillman Water Reclamation Plant, a facility that takes about 70 percent of the sewage from homes and businesses in the San Fernando Valley, runs it through the notoriously pure but uncertain tertiary water-treatment process, and releases 60 million gallons of treated water into the L.A. River each day. *Voilà, the L.A. River is reborn!*

No longer is it a natural ephemeral stream. The river flows all day and night, every day of the year, every year of the century, from here to the ocean. The L.A. River is now a perennial river, which is

*Some say the river begins here at the confluence of Bell and Calabasis Creeks. I say it travels many miles upstream with Bell Creek in the Santa Susana Mountains to the site of a nuclear reactor's meltdown.*

to say that the river is mostly an artificial river, with the exception of seasonal floods of residential stormwater that flows quite copiously from streets and roofs during rainstorms and from sprinkler water overflow. This river is wholly a handmade, hand-watered concoction, with many impurities in its blood. It contains significant quantities of copper, cyanide, bacteria, lead, selenium, nutrients, arsenic, oil, chromium, trash, and unspecified radioactive elements. Remediation of the river is expected to extend for 50 years in some areas, and there are a few existing superfund sites, thanks to the long-held claims of big business to the watershed.

As MacAdams, the guru of the L.A. River, said, "It was originally a seasonal river and now it's a year-round river. Like most post-modern rivers, the L.A. River is a sculpture." He explained that having water in the river helps the richness of the ecosystem and acts to change the extreme loss of riparian areas that California has experienced over the past hundred years. "It's alive with all of the creatures in it," he said, "and with all of the human population increases, we should be thinking about what to do if the city reduces the amount of water in the river. What kind of river do we want? In the end," he added, "I hope it's a gathering place for people."

## Melting down at the beginning

By the time I got to the confluence of Calabasas and Bell Creeks, I was tired of walking along the concrete drainage, cut off at every turn of the creek, so I called my cousin to beg a ride to the top of the drainage. I walked up beside Bell Creek, the add-on portion of the river that isn't much talked about or recognized, and I kept walking down Sherman Way, trying—without success—to keep the creek in sight until Chauncey found me. The drive was spectacular as we wound our way up through the thin, growing developments and open rock drainages into the headwater canyons of Bell Creek.

The Santa Susana Mountains are a knobby range of sedimentary rock formed mostly of shale and sandstone that attain an elevation of 3,700 feet. Several housing developments lie on the lower slopes of this range, but near the summit is the ultimate surprise, or maybe the ultimate insult, in all of Los Angeles: Santa Susana Field Laboratory. This privately owned field station gained fame as the testing site for rocket engines that sent the first U.S. rockets into outer space, NASA's later and wildly successful Apollo space program. It was also the site of a significant nuclear reactor failure in 1959.

Yes, the head of the much-maligned L.A. River drainage was also once the site of a partial nuclear meltdown. In 1959, the main reactor, which was one of ten reactors at the 850-acre site, experienced a partial meltdown that has been compared in danger to the famed 1979 Three-Mile Island meltdown in Pennsylvania. Actually, I learned that the radiation released at the Santa Susana mishap was estimated at 15 to 260 times that released from the Three-

*Riding on a bike path beside the L.A. River.*

Mile Island disaster, according to an April 2006 article in *California Lawyer* magazine. Of the 43 fuel rods, 14 were badly damaged in this experimental sodium-cooled reactor. The reactor provided 75 megawatts of electricity to the local town of Moorpark, which is near the base of the mountain range.

More than 150,000 people live within five miles of the Santa Susana facility, and half a million people live within ten miles, according to *California Lawyer*. In addition, the reactor had no containment, absolutely none, so that much of the nuclear effluvium was sent off as gas or solids into the landscape. Today, little proof remains of what actually happened to the people living downstream of the reactors. Nonetheless, residents of the region were never told about the danger of the laboratory above them as the meltdown occurred. Some individuals were undoubtedly harmed and eventually killed by it. In addition, in the 325 confirmed rocket engine tests (30,000 tests were estimated but unconfirmed), TCE (trichloroethylene) solvents were used. The TCE is still being cleaned up in soil, streambeds, and potentially in the aquifers. A $42 million study by the Environmental Protection Agency in 2012 reported that 10 percent of the field station still contained radioactive concentrations that exceeded background standards. NASA and Boeing were tasked with the cleanup, which was scheduled for completion by 2017.

However, in mid-2020, the Department of Energy (DOE), which is now cleaning up the field laboratory, claimed that they "will continue to work with the state toward processes to remove the remaining

DOE buildings, and toward cleanup of soils and groundwater at the [field laboratory] site." Boeing, the land owner of the field laboratory, wrote in an undated publicity piece that "the transformation of Santa Susanna from field laboratory to open-space is well underway, with native plants and animals reclaiming most of the previously developed areas of the property."

The L.A. River will never be what it was in the 1800s. But it has survived and endured in a place that wanted to make it go away. If you're standing on the riverside when torrential rains fall one fine spring day, as the river floods from the mountains down to Long Beach and your precious belongings become splinters on the banks of this reborn ephemeral stream; when this canal is no longer the sweet, floatable, walkable waterway; when rattlesnakes (those feared and toothy venomous serpents) are once again swept from the San Gabriel Mountains down to Long Beach and your precious property and belongings become fond memories, recall that the river is as unpredictable and remains angrier than a nuclear meltdown. It insists on being remembered like a geological fact.

Remember that the containing walls that engineers hope to make higher are only thin, foolish, and temporary diversions. You will recognize—or perhaps you won't—that this river is not going away. Appease it if you will. Pet it with compliments. Swear at it. Restore it. Walk on it. Piss in it. Respect it. Play in it. Or do what you will with it. But you gotta love it for what it is: the river that created the most beautiful and the most wicked city of Los Angeles in the desert.

# A CAT'S STORY

I was about to head out for a long run along the railroad tracks in Santa Fe last Sunday when I realized that I had left my sunscreen somewhere else. I didn't have any in my backpack, so I stopped a couple that was slowly headed out in their car at the edge of a subdivision and a long wild field of chamisa.

"Excuse me, do you have a little sunscreen that I could borrow?"

They both looked at me and said sorry but, no, they didn't have any. I said thanks and went over by the tracks about 200 feet away and began to stretch my aching old leg muscles in the intense sun. Just then a woman ran out to the car that was now backing from the driveway to the street and she demanded the attention of the drivers. "Hey, hey, hey! Help!" I heard as the car stopped and the driver listened to her frantic pleas.

In 15 seconds a man came out of a nearby house and began screaming at the woman. I couldn't hear what he said, but he certainly got my attention as he screamed at her. The couple in the car were faced by two people, one on either side of their car, as the woman dodged the man around the car's hood. The occupants looked stuck and horrified. The man screamed at the woman across the hood, and she screamed at him in response. I stopped stretching and stood blankly to hear what was said.

He argued in half-articulated words and seemed drunk—drunk on a Sunday morning, a lovely, hot, inviting morning—and he moved to confront the driver of the car. The woman moved away. I walked slowly toward them just as he confronted the driver and banged on the tightly closed window.

"What are you doing here?" he screamed. "Leave us alone and go! Go away! We don't need you!" He pounded on the window again and formed his hand into a form of a gun and pretended to fire it through the window at the people inside. "Go away!"

Astounded, I moved more closely to be a witness and to lend whatever help the people in the car might need. I stood with my arms folded like a disciplinarian, staring at the man and behind him, trying to determine if he had a real gun or was bluffing. I decided it was a bluff, and he turned to stare at me now. The woman took this break in the scene of his attacking her to get into another car, which drove away. I don't know where the other car came from, but it was there at the right moment. The couple drove around the corner and stopped their car. They, too, seemed to be bearing witness.

But that left me facing the angry, drunken man; I backed away as he ranted about something or other. I feared that he might have a real gun in his pocket or somewhere, and it was just the two of us now. I kept my distance from him and backed away.

He saw that their cat was walking my way and said: "Even the fucking cat is going with you." Now he was merely whining and I felt sorry for the man. But not very... I felt more sorry for the cat. And the woman who had left but probably would return. I turned and ran. I ran and waved at the other car in thanks and in a fare-thee-well salute.

I ran for two hours and felt cleaner but very, very tired in the painfully hot sun of the Santa Fe summer. When I returned to the place I had started my run, there was no clue about what had happened or where the people had gone. It seemed as if nothing had happened until the cat came toward me, meowing and meowing, telling its story.

# OF SILENCE AND SANITY

## *Amid Beauty Bleak and Spare*

On my way to Craters of the Moon National Monument, where I intend to view the only eclipse of the sun I'm likely to see, I stop in Carey, Idaho, for a cup of coffee and to see how things have changed there in the past three years. The grocery store that once gathered a hustle and bustle of customers now collects only tumbleweeds, and the sprawling bar just east of town is out of business. Windows are broken in the front rooms of a slightly frumpy motel of cabins, which resembles a motel on Route 66 two decades after the route was changed. But you've got to admire the pluck of Carey's residents in planting an official sign at the edge of town advising, "Carey On!" That, it seems, is the theme of my plan to visit this howling wilderness.

I've visited Craters at least eight times in the past 20 years and seldom has it been easy. Once was for a burial of the monument's former superintendent. Twice on the way to Yellowstone I drove the seven-mile scenic route. But most of my visits to Craters have led me into the black lava land, that pale green sagebrush landscape in a too-hot or too-cold atmosphere drier than a popcorn cooking pot, or to the back side of nowhere, walking this odd land for miles and miles and miles. At some point, when I realized that no place else had the bleakness and spare beauty of Craters of the Moon, it became my kind of place.

I don't expect forgiveness for my mistakes out in this wilderness. Only people forgive here: the place forgives no one, and I've learned to be prepared for anything, as the Boy Scouts say. But if I go in spring, I expect the beauty of flowers and superb lighting. Blazing star flowers bloom an extravagant yellow under the 180-proof sunlight. Hot-pink dwarf monkeyflowers surprise me. I'm soothed by the flawless perfection of tiny bitterroot flowers, the off-white buckwheat flowers that dribble across cinder fields like spilt milk, and the lovely white scablands penstemon that grow out of pure lava like a holy flame of promise. Each is out there if I search, but I usually time my visits in May or early June rather than the midsummer time of this trip.

*Pictured Left: Buckwheat flowers growing on lava in Craters of the Moon National Monument and Preserve.*

The blackness of Craters' night skies has won the distinction of a Silver Tier International Dark Sky Park from the International Dark Sky Association. In the crystalline air, the brilliance of the stars testifies to how the Milky Way was named. The air quality, designated Class 1, won't be allowed by law to degrade. But this also can be a disorienting, deceptive location—for example, when your compass finds north on a magnetic outcrop to the south, or when the seemingly flat, featureless land looks as if it stretches until the end of time but proves to provide rugged terrain 50 feet in front of you. Nights are frigid in winter and days are smacked with heat in the midst of summer, although animals such as bats, owls, snakes, coyotes, deer, antelopes, sage grouse, pikas, and dwarf rabbits do just fine, having found favorable microhabitats.

At the visitors' center, I'm the first person of the day to fill out a permit to hike into the wilderness and camp at Echo Crater. For that matter, so far nobody else has sought a permit for all of the 43,243-acre Craters of the Moon Wilderness within the much larger national monument and preserve. I'm surprised at this because of the hype about the Great American Eclipse happening tomorrow. I fill my backpack with the stuff I'll need to survive and drive the seven-mile route to the farthest end. The wilderness looks just the same as it did last year—it has changed very little since its designation in 1970.

I arrive at the point where the wilderness begins: beyond the modestly developed campsites, the popular and interesting North Crater Trail, the Devils Orchard Nature Trail, the Infernal Cone, all those curious spatter cones, the defined caves, and the absolutely magical Blue Dragon flow to the trailhead. Most people don't get this far, and a number of my Facebook friends criticized me for considering hiking here in August, when the temperatures are soaring, but I figured (correctly) it would mean few tourists. Even so, I've taken my friends' warnings to heart, having brought along two gallons of water for a two-day trip, even if that seemed excessive.

Underfoot is the crackling crunch that makes walking over cinders sound like marching on cereal. I cross the easily walkable Little Prairie to the cirque of Echo Crater, where I can choose among seven fine campsites under the lava cliffs that loom 500 feet high. This crater is not a circular hollow cut in stone by glaciers, the true definition of a cirque. It was created by a massive explosion that cast basalt sky-high, leaving a hole in the ground like a bomb crater. To me, this powerful place embodies the beauty of solitude.

I discovered Echo Crater more than 10 years ago, when I temporarily lost my Brittany spaniel, Camas. Searching for her, I climbed to the top of the crater and saw an Edenic green place far below. I called out my dog's name and heard back, "Camas! Camas! Camas!" Naturally, I immediately liked the name Echo Crater.

Camas and I had hiked here after I had an ischemic stroke in 2000 in a trail-less place in Craters. I was wounded and wanted silence to figure out what having a debilitating stroke could mean. When I felt recovered, I craved the solitude that Craters of the Moon offered—the wilderness was silent and sane.

I had never been a quiet person, but the stroke forced silence and humility upon me, and I went back to reclaim what I'd lost. That year—after I found Camas beside Echo Crater—we walked through a still and rugged ocean of lava. It was a foolish mission to prove that I still could endure the heat of summer as a stroke survivor. Camas dragged and panted as we walked through seemingly endless lava in the 100-degree-plus air temperature, the lava radiating heat in waves above the rock. The heat, surreal and intense, cooked both of us to well done. We came across the merciful shade of a lone and sprawling limber pine, and there we sat. Call it a miracle to find shade in this unforgiving desert or call it luck—we called it a cool place to sleep under a pine tree.

*A limber pine grows in lava.*

We scared a great horned owl from its roost in that pine and it flew out into the hellish day. I wished it luck finding another refuge. I couldn't see one and prayed for its safety, and for ours. Camas drank water from my cup and I from the jug, and we slept in the shade

*The Pioneer
Mountains behind
vegetation in a
kipuka.*

until the temperature dropped. We woke refreshed—if sweating like a wrung-out towel can ever seem refreshed—and walked to the other side of the flow in the northern part of Laidlaw Park. There we found a tremendously fresh array of grasses and a few surviving flowers. Beyond, the aspens of Snowdrift Crater grew keen and vigorous in the deep green of the cool evening shade. We carried on from there to my car. I wondered what on earth we were doing in that oven. Camas slept as I drove, and she didn't hear my apology to her.

Now, on my visit to Echo Crater, the eclipse of the sun will come in the morning. I find the very best camping spot below soaring cliffs in the shade of a grove of tall limber pines. I shelter in a rock stadium that's flat and cool in the midst of the harsh high desert. The quiet of the place seems eerie compared to my city life in Boise, until hornets come buzzing to my campsite. What are they doing here? Water, of course! They need water and my sweat must seem sweet to them, God forbid. They must have come from a source of water, I surmise, but the closest spring, Yellowjacket Waterhole, is a small seep that can serve little more than one of its namesake bugs. I've seen yellowjackets at that bit of water, but it's more than a mile from here.

I put out a dish of water for them, far away from my sleeping spot, which works for a few minutes, until they find the sugar on my trail snacks and return. But all they really need is water and sugar,

and they seem friendly enough. For hornets. I sleep and wake several times in Echo Crater as the day cools and the hornets investigate.

A group of four sage thrashers swoop and land on a nearby rock outcrop. They hop-scotch in the air and land on another boulder. It goes on like this for a minute or so until they see me watching and stop their game. "Silly birds," I call to them. They quickly fly to another set of perches, watch me for a moment or two, and soon become oblivious. Above, about a dozen mourning doves fly in a military formation around the crater and land in an apparent nesting spot on the side of the cliff. They coo and oooh, circle again and again, and fly out of the crater in that same tight formation, as if flung from a sling.

Some years back, I was on the east side of the national monument, amid tall sagebrush and puffs of Great Basin wild rye grasses, when an eclipse of the moon occurred. As the moon appeared and then was slowly effaced by the earth's shadow, the world came to a simple stop without the moon as its partner, and I held my breath without thinking. Then the moon glanced out beyond the shadow and slipped, sliver by sliver, back to its silvery self again. I wondered what the ancient philosophers would have said of the moon disappearing.

On Little Prairie with Echo Crater as my backdrop, I prepare myself for the eclipse of the sun. Little Prairie is a *kipuka* (the

Hawaiian word for "window," I've been told) that runs from the end of the road out beyond Echo Crater. When the Craters of the Moon lava was molten about 2,000 years ago, which is recent in geologic time, Little Prairie lay a bit higher than the flow and thus escaped it. But this prairie was covered in lava much older than that, and by now it has weathered enough to support plants. It's a window into the ecological past isolated from the severe livestock grazing impacts on the Snake River Plain.

There are more than 500 kipukas of various sizes in Craters of the Moon National Monument. In Little Prairie, I've seen gopher snakes, sagebrush lizards, ground squirrels, woodchucks, bats, deer, northern harriers, ravens, doves, and many other birds. Sage

*Oddities live in Craters of the Moon! Beware.*

grouse sign is plentiful. Ecologists have documented an impressive number of species living in Craters: 300 plants, 2,000 insects, 30 mammals, 14 birds, 8 reptiles, and 1 amphibian, the western toad. It's good to know there are places in our world where animals still can live relatively undisturbed by surrounding human impacts.

The next morning, the sun rises and casts a brilliant flame-red glow on the crater's wall, highlighting the chartreuse and saffron colors in a large patch of lichens growing there. Sunlight pours down the lava wall and warms me when it falls to my level. I clutch my cup of coffee with both hands, sip the liquid joyously, and awaken to this quiet light show. Soon I climb to the top of the crater to watch the eclipse.

As I wait for the show to begin, I wander toward a group of trees in the distance. I cross three parallel cracks in the Great Rift, which are roughly 20 to 80 feet deep and about 100 feet wide. Each travels less than a mile, starting and stopping irregularly and continuing on. Together they form a portion of the Great Rift that travels 60 miles in a north–south direction. These cracks indicate a weakness in the Earth's crust and are the origin of many lava flows throughout the region, including several in Craters of the Moon. There are many parallel cracks, some of which hold water and ice tucked in their floors, which is critical information for a person hiking here in the middle of summer. I think the doves must have found water in these cracks when they flew out of Echo Crater.

Reaching the trees, I notice that they stand in a slightly lower place on the land, in a kipuka that might hold a pool of water in rainy times or snow in the spring. In any case, the depression is deep enough for trees to have germinated. A Clark's nutcracker flies from a tree and squawks at me. The bird looks stately in its mantle of gray and black, a white flash of excellence on its tail. These trees must be a summer home for the nutcracker. I root around and find pretty shards of the Blue Dragon flow: the rich cobalt color is from titanium on the surface of the rock as it cooled thousands of years ago. How it shimmers! Magpie that I am, I drop a piece into my pocket, but the better person that I occasionally am pulls it out and throws it back on the ground. The nutcracker watches. They are like that: so judgmental. This one crackles at me—*khaa, khraa, kaaa*—and flies to tell its story to some wizard of the rock.

When the eclipse is roughly 98 percent complete, I walk back to the crater in this abnormal silence. A cool breeze blows and crickets have begun to chirp. The darkness deepens but my shadow remains sharp and I take several photos of burned trees to give the sense of the sunburst effect. In seconds, a sharp light comes from around the sun. The temperature rises and the chirping stops. The only lingering proof of the eclipse is polarized light on limber pines and a bat flying erratically, as bats do, confused at the leaving and coming of sunlight in such a short period.

"Erratic" is a good word for the protection of Craters of the Moon's landscape. In 1924, it was proclaimed as a roughly 54,000-acre national monument by President Calvin Coolidge, with the support of a wild raconteur named Robert Limbert and well-spoken USGS geologist Harold Stearns. They coined the name Craters of the Moon, giving the area rhetorical pizazz and a look-to-the-sky sort of appeal. Limbert lobbied for the monument designation in Washington, D.C., and wrote a spirited article for *National Geographic*, which added strong public support for protection of the area.

The smaller wilderness area within the national monument was designated in 1970, and then in 2000, a proclamation by President Bill

Clinton expanded the national monument to a seemingly endless sea of 750,000 acres of lava and kipukas. A few years later, the area was legislatively redesignated as a combined national monument and national preserve, which acknowledged the opinions of ranchers and motorized vehicle users. The bill was passed by the U.S. Congress and signed by the president, giving it more full-bodied support than that of a simple presidential proclamation.

Within the monument and preserve are thousands of acres of wilderness study areas (WSAs), which contain mostly pure lava with a few acres of grasslands that easily could be supported for their wilderness qualities by the state legislature and the U.S. Congress. A WSA is a Bureau of Land Management category of land management. Each WSA is being studied for wilderness designation, and until that study is complete, no actions can be advanced to diminish its wilderness value. WSAs do not have a clear management purpose, which means until Congress acts on their behalf, they can be managed only as pseudo-wilderness.

When I think of wilderness, what first comes to mind is the wicked land in Craters of the Moon. I was gladdened and surprised by the Idaho Legislature's support of a plan for the original 54,000-acre national monument to be turned into a national park. The land would get better funding for campgrounds, interpretation, road repairs, wilderness management, scientific studies, collaborative meetings, and outreach publicity. The closest communities, such as Carey and Arco, would get the benefits of increased visitation to a national park, which always draws more interest than a national monument. I hope it will give businesses in Carey and Arco a glimmering chance of survival, while designating more wildernesses in Idaho.

Craters of the Moon is a unique place on our planet. In its razor-sharp lava, in its infinite but broken blackness, in its solitude and the stark splendor of cinder cones, in the twilit caves and naturally formed rock bridges, in that mystical Blue Dragon flow, but most of all in the delicacy of the plants and in the animals that eke out their lives there, it is unique. In all of this, there is beauty. Plus, wonderful stories endure of people who fought against the lava while traveling to settle Idaho and Oregon. I believe that care for Craters demands we protect all of the existing species of plants and animals in that dry environment, even while we wisely interpret its weird volcanic history,

Echo Crater in
Craters of the Moon
National Monument
and Preserve.

invite tourists into the region, and help communities around Craters to survive in a tough economy.

There are many odd tales to tell about Craters, some of them equal parts comical and wonderful, some of them akin to lies that have never been debunked. But what do you or I really know about the Bridge of Tears, Amphitheater Cave, Vermillion Chasm, the sad story of Kings Bowl, the Alice in Wonderland curiosity that might be found in a trip to Lasso Cave, or the almost comical Bridge of the Moon? All we can do is go, learn—and be careful in Craters of the Moon, where more than one person has died out in the elements. Nevertheless, as the nearby townsfolk would have it, we simply need to "Carey On!"

# A DAY IN THE SLAMMER

About the time I was fingerprinted, I realized my jail sentence was for real. Before that moment it just seemed like some kind of lousy practical joke. "Oh, come on," I felt like saying, "one day in jail for not having auto insurance? What's that supposed to prove? Isn't the $80 fine enough?" But there I stood, transferring ink from a piece of Masonite to a pair of official-looking cards and leaving behind my unique smudges.

"It's no big deal. Really," the officer assured me. "Fingerprints are overrated. One set of prints goes to the Valley County records and the other to the FBI." No big thing? Who is *he* kidding? I felt pretty low about being a part of official police records.

"Isn't this a bit ridiculous for a one-day sentence?" I asked. He snapped a picture of me standing beside a scale of inches to determine my height, with my arms crossed and my hands visible on my shoulders. My finest convict pose! He did not argue my question. "Does this even cover the cost of booking a person for a day in jail?

"Hardly."

It occurred to me that the vast majority of people in this country have never been to jail, and until last week, I was a member of that majority with no intention of parting company. But two weeks ago I managed to have a minor automobile accident, which I insisted upon reporting to the police.

The accident was no big deal really, but my lack of insurance put me in court on the following Monday. In court I learned the maximum penalty for not having insurance was $500 and six months in jail. Egad! That seemed a bit extravagant! It did make my current sentence feel like a gift, however absurd.

Prior to being fingerprinted, I had to be booked. Bron Day, the jailer, and a kind man of intelligence and wit, asked me if I would like to make a telephone call, wrote a description of me, and took all my loose belongings—keys, pocket change, and jewelry. He also gave me a prison rulebook filled with do's and don'ts. The rulebook made it clear that I had few rights aside from eating, sleeping, and breathing. Beyond that there were privileges. Long-term inmates get a television; we all were entitled to exercise and sunshine five days a week, we may buy candy bars and cigarettes from the prison commissary, and we may have visitors and phone calls during certain hours.

I signed a few papers, then went to trade street clothes for jailbird attire. Bron gave me a stylish black V-neck smock and baggy black pants like those worn by surgeons. He also issued one sheet, a thin mattress pad and cover, one blanket, one towel, a toothbrush, toothpaste, a small bar of Ivory soap, socks, and sandals. He told me to take a shower and put on my new clothes and led me to the shower stall in a vacant cell.

Having already showered that morning, I suggested that I didn't need another. "Either you take a shower or I have to strip search you," he said, smiling. Not knowing what a strip search involved, and not wanting to find out, I opted for the shower. Bron handed me some liquid soap, which called itself "the gentle iodine" and smelled like a waltz in the hospital. He suggested I get wet. The showerhead pelted me with a hundred or so tiny needles of water, which soon left me feeling like I'd waded naked through a jungle of stinging nettle.

I put on the jail clothes and Bron escorted me, feeling like a generic convict, to my cell. He introduced me to my cellmate who was reading *Papillon* and smoking a cigarette. A fleeting thought crossed my mind that I might have requested a non-smoking cell room with a better view, but I let that thought flee. Fortunately, my cellmate was not a violent delinquent but turned out to be a very balanced fellow. He was halfway through his 24-hour sentence for carrying no auto insurance and was beginning to go stir crazy.

The cell itself was an extreme version of a one-room efficiency apartment with its two cast iron cots, a sink, a toilet, and a very handy shower stall. The cell was probably 10 × 12 feet and was decorated with two themes in mind: Austerity and Security.

Three walls and the ceiling were concrete painted a Pepto-Bismol color, while the fourth wall was made of metal bars. The barred wall overlooked a corridor where the prison guards could walk to keep an eye on the prisoners in each cell. The floor was concrete painted battle-ship gray. The cell was immaculate to the extent that my bare feet gathered no dirt. Everything was immobile except for a small round-topped wrought iron table. I was thinking: good! I could commit suicide! The door to freedom had a 5- × 10-inch window cut in at eye level, and a somewhat larger trapdoor which opened up wide enough for a food tray to be slipped into the cell. All in all, not a very homey place.

My first meal, lunch, was the equivalent of a budget airplane meal. It was well balanced and tolerable. Apparently the regular cook didn't work weekends. The rules said: "You are expected to eat your meals!" So I did. Far be it for me to buck authority. I also chose two candy bars from the commissary. The commissary is a carton of varied candy bars which Bron held up to the 5- × 10-inch window. I paid a buck each for the candy bars, the price being deducted from the $5 I had left in my clothes. I just initialed an account card. Room service was never so handy nor a credit card so casual. I might find myself liking it here.

While driving to the jail that morning, I had hoped for rain. I harbored the selfish thought that if my day was ruined, everyone else's should also be ruined. Later the jail was shaken by thunder. The lights flickered off and on three times. The smell of rain dampened the earth and sucked through the ventilation system and into my cell. It made me feel good to know what the weather was doing outside, even if I couldn't see it. When thunder stopped, I wondered if sun was shining through glorious clouds. Nothing is more beautiful than sunshine after rain—rainbows, mist, earth and water smells, the colors so remarkably fresh.

I regretted being in the jail cell and missing these things and I envied my friends being caught in the rain. A light outside the bars cast shadows across my concrete ceiling like rays of sunlight through the clouds, reminding me of my predicament.

My cellmate said this was assuredly the longest day of his life. When he was released, I had no one to talk with and boredom expanded. I read a book cover to cover and fell to boredom again. The only outside stimulus came from the next cell over. There, some man blew his nose like a trombone, or made noise urinating, or turned the TV louder. I tried to imagine what he looked like. Was he a trombone? But even that got boring.

When it's not frightening, jail must be the most boring place in the world. It is easy to dwell on time there and impossible to accurately judge its passing. I was glad to sleep when the lights went out. Next thing I knew, lights flashed on to announce morning. Well, it wasn't exactly the next thing I knew, as sleeplessness lingered on through the night in dreamlike drips and drops of "Where the hell am I?" Bron slid a hearty breakfast through the trap door, making me feel like someone's dog, but the meal was most excellent. After breakfast Bron announced that I had to leave.

My own clothes felt wonderful! The sky was blue and flecked with clouds when I walked outside of the drab building. My heart soared. I almost felt foolish feeling so good. After all, I'd only spent one day in captivity. But being cooped up in a small room with no freedom and all of my choices being made by others for even a small time was claustrophobic to the sensibility of who I was. I'm not quite sure what the lesson of all this may be, but I promise you that my car is now insured.

# HOME

Fifteen Canada geese are flying south, honking like a traffic jam. Ospreys have already flown to the coastal states along the same route they took last year, following rivers mostly for meals of fish. Gone, too, are mountain bluebirds, scarlet tanagers, and goldfinch, all of which have flown over the mountains in sparks of colored light. I haven't seen black bear or gray wolves on my property outside McCall, Idaho, for two years, but I know they're out there.

The apple trees haven't been raided this year, as they were two years ago by a bear, and the golden green fruits lie rotting on the ground or are saved in a bowl inside my "shabin." Soon, a small herd of elk will pass across my land, taking the same route they've traveled for as long as I've been here, on their route to a higher, safer landscape, away from bullet-riddled hunting grounds.

Two summers ago, as I heard wolves howl throughout the night, their songs sent shivers up my back that both warned and soothed me. The wolves apparently got too close to a band of domestic sheep being herded along Farm-to-Market Road. As a result, the next night, I heard a helicopter as it hovered for half an hour, not far north of my land. This was an exceptionally odd sound—an aggressive, military sound—to hear in my rural environment. I knew that the Fish and Wildlife Service hired pilots to track and kill or anesthetize and move "problem wolves," and with the state of Idaho now having authority over wolf management, they would kill the wolves for sheep ranchers. I couldn't say if the wolves I had heard were considered a problem for sheep ranchers; nor did I know whether the chopper was hired by the agency to control those wolves. But I haven't heard a wolf since. They're gone. Two days after that incident, I drove slowly behind a massive herd of sheep—perhaps 500—for at least a mile, cursing the sheep for getting in the way of the inspiring but problem wolves. I understood what had happened and was saddened by the loss of wolves in my neighborhood, because they had been extirpated for many decades prior; but the Pollyanna in me wanted the wolves to escape, though the evidence suggested otherwise.

These are the circumstances I recall as I pack up my shabin, getting ready to move out to a rented house in Boise. This new place will be a wintering place and possibly more. It has become too expensive to live in McCall, at least for an aging writer facing another harsh winter in Valley County.

Perhaps you're wondering, what is a shabin? It is part shack, part cabin, a shabin—a place that developers might call a "teardown palace," a ramshackle, ticky-tacky hut, a place uninhabitable for any sane person throughout winter. But of course it all depends on your perspective, for this place has sheltered me for five years. Around me, property owners have deserted their nice homes and lives, bailing out from under heavy loans or mortgages for obvious financial threats. For what it's worth, I have no crushing debts, but I have some small, nagging obligations that I

*Mike's shabin.*

can't afford to pay without a consistent job, and jobs in McCall have been inconsistent for awhile. Selling this land will allow me some spare money to breathe for a change and to think about the future.

My one-room shabin was approved by Valley County with a five-dollar storage unit building permit. Although it isn't quite legal for me to live here, I have built a composting toilet in an outhouse and installed solar panels for lights, music, and a well pump. The well was drilled some 50 years ago and had been capped until I opened it three years ago and tapped its pure water.

I built the shabin for about $5,000—it's not pretty but it's serviceable. Any good carpenter could make the shabin into a more "kindly" cabin by adding siding atop the hardboard plywood and covering the inside insulation with nicer boards. Along with some good friends, I built this place with muscle, beer, and kindness: putting piers under the floor, tilting up the walls, lifting rafters and attaching them to the walls, roofing the top, adding a front door salvaged from a torn-down jewelry building in town, installing windows to the eastern view, a loft, countertop, furniture, and wood stove—all of this created through friendship, labor, and shared beer. Over these five years, this shabin has been my writing retreat. My girlfriend lives a few miles away, and her home has been my home about half the time.

The land upon which this shabin was built has taught me more than I've learned in all my years of traditional work. For 24 years, I've worked to transform this land from an overgrazed horse and cattle lot to a natural place with tall grasses and encroaching forests. It is now in the process of transitioning from an area where 85-foot-tall Ponderosa pines once grew, into an area where 85-foot Ponderosas will again grow. After the big trees were harvested by a former owner, shade-intolerant lodgepole pines filled the void.

These smaller pines have provided the shade in which Ponderosa pines are again growing. Now, the lodgepole pines are experiencing an infestation of bark beetles, and many of them are dying, enabling the Ponderosa pines—now that they've reestablished—to grow without competition.

Aspen trees are expanding into the forest and beginning to cover the open land that had been used for livestock grazing. They grow in several groups of identical clones; each individual grove follows a different "time-clock," with leaves changing to classic autumnal colors, from green to gold, orange to scarlet, in turn. The shifting colors last for several weeks, and as the groves are beginning to grow together, the colors blend. I would never have noticed this had I not owned my land for so many years.

Grasses growing on the neighbor's land, which has been grazed lightly for many years, run along the fence, enclosing the cattle-free land on my side. Here the difference between our two properties is stark, as the grazed land shows many small patches of bare soil and shorter grasses. On my side of the fence, the vegetation is dense. I have reached the conclusion that vegetation on the rancher's side is more diverse than what grows on my side. On my side, the grasses haven't been chewed down and the roots have established themselves in thick mats, giving other plants little opportunity to grow.

On the other side, where the livestock tramples and eats the grass, other plants can grow on the bare ground, and that has increased the number of different plants that can survive in the spring when the ground is still damp. I now realize that to increase the diversity on my land, it needs to be grazed by elk, deer or, heaven forbid, domestic cows or sheep, and it should be burned occasionally, so that other flowering plants can live here.

However, the price of bringing in cows or sheep to my property is that these invasive animals would displace the wildlife that I love. I've been an environmentalist since 1984 and have worked with a number of organizations at a number of levels, and this is not what I would have thought when I once fought logging and grazing on public lands. But time has mellowed me. A little. Not a lot, actually. But time tells me to move on from this land and tackle other challenges. I will get my book published with the money from this property, which I have worked on since having a stroke in 2000. These dreams have moved so damned slowly! As slowly as the growing bit of wisdom, the recovery of this land, and the nature of my heart. My home is not built on a piece of land or on the memories of it, but in the ever-changing wholeness of my experiences of living.

# A FOOL'S DRUNKEN PILGRIMAGE
## IN SEARCH OF A GILA MONSTER

I went to the Gila River in Southwest New Mexico on a search for a Gila monster in late April when I lived in Santa Fe. I was thinking of my father, who had invested in a lemon ranch in Arizona, and a story he had told me about a Gila monster he'd seen many years before as it ran though the ranch. He was surprised by its odd, colorful bearing, its tubbiness, and he was told that it was poisonous. Its poisonness made it much more glamorous to me when I was a kid and that hadn't diminished a'tall when I grew up. I researched the lizard at the University of New Mexico in Albuquerque and learned that Gila monsters are rarely seen but when they bite with their vice-like jaws, they don't give up easily. They chew on the victim so that the poison sinks in. The monsters scared and fascinated me and so I went looking for a story about the famed Gila monsters beside the Gila River. I mean, that made sense, right? That's where I thought they should live.

I figured that I wouldn't find one on my quest for the monster, but what the heck, I might, I was game. It was a curiosity and an excuse to get out of Santa Fe. I talked to a biologist working at REI in Santa Fe as I got maps for the southern part of the state where the Gila River ran. When I purchased the maps, she suggested that I visit a place outside Silver City, New Mexico: Turkey Creek, where she saw one last year. This was an amazing piece of luck: an out-of-work biologist, salesperson at REI who had done research on my lizards in New Mexico! She was my kinda gal. But she had to work and I had to travel a bit, so I went alone.

I talked to everyone I could find, well, in the bars around Santa Fe and asked if they knew where a Gila monster lived. Well, it was a good pickup line, but no one knew where I could see a Gila monster, although one woman pointed across the bar to the man she called a poisonous reptile. Santa Fe was kinda boring and a bit high-brow for me to hang out looking for single women to dance with or drinking $10 beers to get drunk, so I took off to Silver City and looked for a drunk or two to ask about Gila monsters. I found one in a bar in Silver City who said, "Sure, I know where you can find a Gila monster because I've seen many of them."

"Yeh, right," I said.

"No, ser-riou-sly, you go down to the Gila River and walk into the Gila Wilderness and along the river you will see Gila monsters laying on the rocks beside the river. They are practically littering the river banks." He laughed loudly, almost manically. Damn drunks. I drank my next Budweiser beer, which was refreshingly cheap. That sounded like a tall tale, like the guy had changed the story from one with bikinis on the beach in Santa Monica to one that fit the thing I wanted to see, but you know, whatever, I had nothin' better to do than wander through this two-bit town on a quest for Gila monsters. However, the wilderness was up the Gila River from the point that he put his finger on, not downstream, where I was headed. This man was a sham.

Another person said she hadn't seen one and suggested going to search in Arizona. A third guy thought that they should be in New Mexico, probably around the Gila Wilderness, but he was more interested in making a pathetic pool table shot and made one that landed up sending the cue ball off the table and into the lap of the drunken woman I had talked to. She cursed and threw the pool pall back at him. I told him that in my bar, in McCall, Idaho, that move wouldda cost him five bucks and he should buy a beer for the woman he'd hit. "Good thing we're not in Idaho, Toto," he drawled, and continued to mess up another shot. New Mexico is a big place so I just thanked him, took his free beer, and headed out to the Gila River after sleeping in my car on the edge of an expansive arroyo. It was a crap shoot to head out for the river, but I had a cold cup of coffee as proof of my sobriety last night and drove through an absolutely wonderful hangover.

I walked along the Gila River and combed the rocky banks for the elusive Gila monster, feeling like I was on a goddamned snipe hunt for several hours. I looked high and low calling out for my monster. "Where are you little buddy?" Then I crossed an ancient water diversion and went up a slim arroyo that was full of big boulders and channels that water had built. It looked, well, kind of monsterish with enormous rocks cast all about. And lo, about half an hour upstream I looked before me and there was a Gila monster lollygagging across the gravel bar. Talk about luck; I almost stepped on it! I was incredulous and extremely excited to see this foot-and-a-half long poisonous lizard that my father had told me about 40 years ago, crawling right before my eyes! That's a Gila monster. That is a goddamned Gila monster! Is body was as svelte as a sausage; its color was orange-and-Pepto-Bismol-pink with stark black bands across its bee-bee studded body. Its tail was thick as an old man's thumb and its thick, black tongue slipped in and out of its wide mouth to taste the world, sensing it like a rattlesnake's tongue. The Gila monster seemed a prehistoric character out of a comic book or a portrait from the artists in Santa Fe on Canyon Road. It just didn't seem real. And here it was: a prize right out of a fool's drunken pilgrimage.

I watched it for two hours during which he or she ate a bird's egg under a bush that I'd scared it to. It swallowed the whole damned egg after chewing on it for a couple of bites and found it impossible to break. What the hell, Lizzie, go for it: always eat more than you can swallow. I figured that my bothering it had resulted in its getting the egg, so I figured that we each had a good experience. My quest weekend was cut short by finding the very subject of my quest, the lizard that I'd only dreamed to find, as if on a peyote voyage. I wasn't supposed to find it. I had more looking to do, more wandering, more hiking for the weekend and now this. I found it. End of story. I swear to God, my father was there looking at me from somewhere above or below. He laughed at the sight of this venomous and beautiful lizard that I actually found. Maybe he planted it.

However, my quest weekend had other high points: pronghorn antelope running along the road racing me in my car, a large domineering rattlesnake crawling slowly across my trail, and a stunningly gorgeous mountain kingsnake along another road with red, white, and yellow bands on it. However, of all the oddball things I found along the roads in and around Silver City, that Gila monster was the best thing that Earth Day in April could provide me with: a mythic animal that was out on the earth and very, very much alive. We left in peace, that sweet little monster and I; it went one way and I, back home to Santa Fe. But I heard that warm laugh of my long dead father in that hot, hot sun along the Gila River and that made my soul fly.

# THE ART OF WAR AND WILDERNESS

*Defining the Fate of Idaho's Boulder-White Clouds Wilderness*

O nce upon a time, all of Idaho's forests were green, water ran gin-clear from the mountains, the sky was not cloudy all day, and there was no need for wilderness designations. But in the 1940s, '50s, and early '60s, people like Mardy Murie, Bob Marshall, Howard Zahniser, Aldo Leopold, Sigurd Olson, and Wallace Stegner felt compelled to insist that the last remaining wild places in the United States be protected. Logging, mining, and road building were rampant and wildlands were being diminished like "snow on a hot summer's day," as conservationist John Muir once said.

Shortly before his death in 1964, Zahniser wrote, "I believe we have a profound fundamental need for areas of the earth where we stand without our mechanisms that make us immediate masters over our environment." That same year, President Lyndon Johnson signed into law the Wilderness Act, which was written by Zahniser, and 9.1 million acres were immediately designated. In those days, all of society seemed to look forward to a four-day workweek, and with less work to occupy our time, we needed wilderness. Now, in 2015, neither wilderness nor a shortened workweek affords much certainty.

## A monument or wilderness?

Last week, two Idaho congressmen, U.S. Representative Mike Simpson and Senator Jim Risch, introduced the Sawtooth National Recreation Area and Jerry Peak Wilderness Additions Act, a bill that would designate 275,665 acres of wilderness in three areas of the Boulder-White Cloud Mountains. This bill has been in discussion for 30 years, but the current proposal, a recrafted version of Simpson's CIEDRA (Central Idaho Economic Development and Recreation Act) legislation, which would have designated 332,928 acres in the Boulder-White Clouds, is much smaller than other plans proposed over the years. The legislation shrank the area

*Pictured Left: Castle (left) and Merriam (right) peaks in the White Cloud Mountains in Sawtooth National Recreation Area of Sawtooth National Forest, Idaho.*

PHOTO: FREDLYFISH4, WIKIMEDIA COMMONS

by some 60,300 acres over several days of recent discussions with snowmobile and heli-skiing interests. Compromises have been traded for a dozen years, including attempts to win support from Risch, who is said to have blocked the last version of the bill in the Senate. Will this be the bill?

The new Boulder-White Clouds Wilderness bill allows more land to be used by off-road vehicles and snowmobilers by eliminating some roadless land from wilderness designation, but it defines fewer exceptions to wilderness under the Wilderness Act, making the areas smaller while gaining begrudging support from some wilderness purists.

Simpson and Risch introduced their wilderness bill shortly after they heard that President Barack Obama would proclaim the Boulder-White Cloud Mountains a national monument. That was a frightening and nebulous proposal that worried many of their constituents in Central Idaho. The national monument was said to protect the ecosystem overlaying the Boulder-White Cloud Mountains, but it didn't define exactly what that protection entailed. It could mean anything, and the president had the power to protect the land under the Antiquities Act of 1906 by proclamation. The Obama administration believed the proclamation could be accomplished before anyone really knew what it would do. It would be *fait accompli* in a year, and that threat prompted snowmobile supporters and off-road vehicle users to react. In 2014, 95 percent of the voters who voted in Custer County, which is adjacent to the Boulder-White Cloud Mountains, opposed the national monument designation.

"We do need wilderness," Sandra Mitchell, public lands director of the Idaho State Snowmobile Association told me in February. "It is not a completely bad idea; however, I believe there is enough wilderness in Idaho." Mitchell is a veteran of the "wilderness wars" of the 1980s and '90s and was an aide to former Senator Steve Symms, a Republican. Consequently, she is careful with her words but pretty clear on her message.

Before about 1998, logging and mining were viewed as the biggest conflicts with regard to roadless areas, but today logging in Idaho is only a small percentage of what it was in 1990, and mining has many more regulations attached to it after years of environmental litigation and wrangled-out compromises. Today the issues in the Boulder-White Cloud Mountains are mostly recreation-based conflicts.

John Podesta, known as the knuckle-rapping master for the Obama administration and counselor to the president, gave Simpson six to nine months to get his bill passed before Obama would move on the national monument idea. Lindsey Slater, Simpson's chief of staff, said that the congressman "wouldn't have suggested the bill if he thought that he couldn't get it done before the monument would be declared." Slater said that Simpson had "met with the affected groups and he continues to push for a bill that works for everyone. We think that an Idaho-based solution would be better than a Washington, D.C., plan."

"There are a lot of compromises in Simpson's bill," said Dani Mazzotta, Central Idaho Director for the Idaho Conservation League (ICL). "It's tough, and over a decade it has been getting smaller every time we see it. We don't oppose it, but we're disappointed in the trade-offs that are being made now. However, the national monument proposal has legs and strong support." As she said, a national monument does not protect wilderness. Mazzotta added that she thought that "President Obama will listen to all interests. It will be pretty balanced. The big thing is that ICL will continue to support the national monument and build more support for it." Compromise is the name of the game in Idaho politics.

## Is the Boulder-White Clouds National Monument a viable plan?

It's unclear exactly what the national monument would protect. Nonetheless, everyone has big plans for it. Call it the president's "smorgasbord proclamation," a political compromise favoring the president and his supporters. The proclamation would most likely support mountain bikes in roadless areas recommended by the Forest Service as wilderness, would support the concept of wilderness, and probably would offer snowmobiles and off-road vehicles a number of routes within the monument's approximately 600,000 acres.

The Simpson and Risch wilderness bills would create three new wilderness areas that exclude mountain bikes and motorized vehicles and that allow adjacent roadless areas to be managed for other uses. The wilderness areas that would be designated under Simpson's legislation are the Hemingway-Boulders Wilderness (67,998 acres), the White Clouds Wilderness (90,769 acres), and the Jim McClure-Jerry Peak Wilderness (116,898 acres).

The Snowmobile Association's Mitchell laughed when asked whether she supported the national monument or Simpson's bill. "It's not a decision that the recreation coalition ever envisioned. But it is our reality now and we are working on it. We've worked on the monument proposal and we've put together excellent material. We went to D.C. to meet with the Under Secretary [of the U.S. Department of Agriculture], to CEQ [Council on Environmental Quality], and to the Pew Foundation. We've taken our message and we've told folks how we feel about the monument. I've done everything but crying big, and if I thought that would make a difference I'd cry!" Mitchell would gain more out of Simpson's wilderness bill because much of the land that is used by snowmobiles or off-road vehicles was eliminated from the wilderness. That was not the case in earlier versions of CIEDRA.

According to a 2010 Congressional Research Service report on national monuments, the Antiquities Act requires designation of "the smallest area compatible with the proper care and management of the objects to be protected." But that statement has been interpreted rather liberally over the years. Consider the 1.9 million-acre Grand Staircase-Escalante National Monument in which, with the stroke of his pen, President Bill Clinton zeroed out a very valuable coal mine and supported a huge recreation industry. In Alaska, President Jimmy Carter, with the support of his Interior Secretary Cecil Andrus (another Idahoan), reserved 100 million acres of land, which led to a negotiation protecting 56 million acres of wilderness, national parks, and national refuges. That negotiation process also opened up other areas for specific purposes such as logging and oil production. Carter said that he had been forced to use the Antiquities Act by Congress' failure to act in a reasonable time to deal with the land issue in Alaska.

Those are exactly the circumstances today in Idaho: Congress hasn't acted in a responsible period of time to deal with Central Idaho's public lands. Simpson has attempted to pass legislation since 2004 on the Boulder-White Cloud Mountains, the crème de la crème of Idaho's unprotected mountain ranges. Legions of Congress members have considered the issue of Idaho's roadless areas since 1986 (Representatives John Seiberling, Peter Kostmayer, Bruce Vento, Larry LaRocco, Morris Udall, and Senators James McClure, Steve Symms, and Larry Craig, among them). No decision could be made on the roadless forested areas in Idaho, and advocates for wilderness faced off against advocates for logging, mining, and grazing. A report put together with funding from the state of Idaho in the 1990s recommended against deciding on the wilderness issue because wilderness designation was too contentious. And there it has lingered and festered over the years.

The Antiquities Act was designed to protect federal lands and resources quickly; presidents of both political parties have used it to proclaimed monuments. Many of the 178 created monuments have been controversial; some have been converted to national parks, national reserves, or other categories; and none of the proclamations needed to follow environmental laws, including the National Environmental Policy Act (NEPA). NEPA normally requires time-consuming and costly environmental impact statements to justify significant changes to the environment.

The Antiquities Act was used by President George W. Bush in 2009 to create the 61-million-acre Marianas Trench Marine National Monument near Guam. In 1908, Theodore Roosevelt used it to create the Grand Canyon National Monument, and in 1933, President Herbert Hoover created the 2-million-acre Death Valley National Monument. Grand Canyon and Death Valley national monuments have been expanded and converted into national parks since then. In 1987, President Ronald Reagan used the act to create the El Malpais National Monument in New Mexico, and in 2000, President Clinton expanded the Craters of the Moon National Monument in Idaho. Obama has designated 16 national monuments, including, most recently, Pullman National Monument in Chicago, the Honouliuli National Monument near Pearl Harbor on Oahu, the Bears Ears National Monument in Utah, and the Browns Canyon National Monument in Colorado.

It seems that Simpson's worries about a national monument being proclaimed in Idaho are well founded. But he knows well the

*Frog Lake in the White Cloud Mountains.*

political strategies in the art of war and wilderness. One political sleight-of-hand may be used to change an Idaho national monument into some other land protection category through legislation following its proclamation, as Simpson did with the Craters of the Moon National Monument and Reserve. That national monument became, in part, a legislated national reserve. And the law affirming it assured that off-road vehicle advocates could continue to use Craters of the Moon, contingent upon a travel plan being developed.

Another complication is that Senator Mike Crapo and Senator Risch introduced Senate Bill 228 (S. 228), the National Monument Designation Transparency and Accountability Act, in January, which would make the process of proclaiming a national monument far more difficult than it is now. That bill would require the approval of Congress and legislation in the state where the national monument is proposed before any monument can be approved. It would also require compliance with NEPA. Anger over President Franklin Roosevelt's 1943 creation of the Jackson Hole National Monument altered implementation of the Antiquities Act in Wyoming; it required the support of Congress for any national monument crafted by the president in that state, and the provision proved effective in eliminating presidential power over national monuments there.

Passage of S. 228 or inserting it into other legislation would likely have the same effect in Idaho, or elsewhere if it is universal. However, Obama would most likely veto it.

## Wilderness in the White Clouds? Not so much? Or maybe just a little?

After passage of the Wilderness Act, the U.S. Forest Service created a nationwide roadless area policy that considered all of the unroaded Forest Service lands. Conservationists challenged that policy twice, and the land under study increased both times. Congress sought to resolve the wilderness issue in 1986 by designating 8.6 million acres in 20 states, and in those states the designations largely succeeded. However, many Western states, including Idaho, were left in the lurch with outstanding roadless areas in contention for wilderness designation by 2015, when Idaho had roughly 9 million acres of roadless areas, in addition to 4.5 million acres that were already designated as wilderness. Moreover, the Bureau of Land Management's organic law was amended in 1976 and protected all of the inventoried unroaded lands in that agency's desert land as wilderness study areas (WSAs). Every WSA, of which there were 1.8 million acres in Idaho, was protected not by a mere policy as the Forest Service had done, but specifically by the Federal Lands Policy and Management Act (FLPMA), until they were studied and "released" from, or protected, as wilderness.

With 4.5 million acres of wilderness areas, Idaho is currently in third place in the 50 states for the amount of designated wilderness, behind Alaska's 57 million acres and California's 15 million acres. There are now 109.5 million acres of designated wilderness in the United States. Idaho still has about 11 million acres of wild, unroaded land that qualify as wilderness out of a total of 53 million acres of land in the state. And 8.5 percent of the state has been designated as wilderness under the Wilderness Act, including the Frank Church River of No Return, Selway-Bitterroot, Gospel-Hump, Sawtooth, Craters of the Moon, Hells Canyon (Seven Devils area), and Owyhee River wilderness areas. Is 8.5 percent—some 4.5 million acres— enough wilderness for a state that has another 11 million acres of undeveloped land?

In his recent guest opinion in the *Idaho Statesman*, Eric Melson, former program director of the Selway-Bitterroot Frank Church Foundation, wrote the following:

> The traditional conservation demographic has shifted. Instead of just backpackers, hunters, anglers, boaters, and climbers speaking up for healthy landscapes, mountain bikers are voicing their concern about access to and protection of America's wild places. Adrenalin-fueled activities piloted by younger activists should now have a seat at the table.... National monument status is sensical, does not need legislative approval, and has room to negotiate travel panning for all parties, especially mountain bikers.

That states the position of the *nouveau* advocates for mountain bikes on the national monument for Idaho, but it fails to account for the political element of wilderness designations.

In fact, in March 2015 Simpson stated, "Allowing corridors in the three proposed wilderness areas is non-negotiable, and the three wildernesses in my bill will each remain undivided and without corridors. I am certain that anything else will result in a monument."

Brad Brooks, deputy regional director for the Wilderness Society, took a different twist: "We are not working on a wilderness bill for the Boulder-White Clouds," he said. "It's all been talk, and talk is cheap. The proof is in the pudding. It's not a Congress that we think will support a lot of wilderness." the Wilderness Society, the Idaho Conservation League, the Wood River Bicycle Coalition, and the International Mountain Biking Association have formed a firm agreement, signed as a memorandum of understanding, committing them to work on the proposed national monument.

Brooks laid out the plan for the monument, which he termed was "a very real and credible proposal that has the attention of the president and the administration.... We've created a coalition of support that is quite broad: recreation groups, elected officials, sportsmen organizations and conservation groups. One of the things that I like about the monument is the watershed protection. But what makes the Boulder-White Clouds special is the people, uses, and the land itself."

Brooks mentioned that the East Fork of the Salmon River has the longest migration route for anadromous fish and the highest elevation spawning habitat for salmon and steelhead. "It also includes the entire East Fork of the Salmon River drainage, allows a variety of recreation uses from mountain bikers to hunters, and all of them would have a place in the monument." The monument may include comprehensive protections for the region's wildlife, fisheries, wild lands, recreation, and historic values, and a management plan would determine where mechanized and motorized vehicle use would be permitted.

Gary Macfarlane, director of Friends of the Clearwater in Moscow, Idaho, presented his organization's perspective: "Both proposals have problems, and I find a lot of irony in them. There is less mountain biking allowed in certain places than in the monument. That's weird, and making a deal with the mountain bikers is a strategic blunder." Macfarlane's group supports 1.5 million acres of wild areas in North Idaho. "The wilderness bill is too small, but it's better than anything I've seen before, because it doesn't include all of the special language that CIEDRA had. It's the cleanest wilderness language bill that we've seen from Simpson; it's cleaner than what passed in the River of No Return Wilderness Bill in 1980."

George Nickas, executive director of Wilderness Watch, concurs with Macfarlane. He has worked for more than 20 years at maintaining the quality of designated wilderness areas and runs a national organization supporting that work. He said, "The national monument proposal eviscerates the land with all of the ORV [off-road vehicle] and mountain bike paths. Simpson's bill provides wilderness, and it doesn't mandate a bunch of crap like it once did. I think that the land in Simpson's current bill would be better protected than it would be under a monument. But the protected land should be about twice as big."

Regardless of all of the disagreement, the Wilderness Act defines a wilderness as an area "where the earth and its community of life are untrammeled by man, where man himself is a visitor who does not remain... [It] retain[s] its primeval character and influence, without permanent improvements or human habitation, which is protected and managed so as to preserve its natural conditions." When the law passed in 1964, it allowed grazing, hiking, river boating, and horseback riding, but no motorized vehicles or bicycles, and it allowed each state to manage its wildlife. There were other compromises in specific areas, and in the River of No Return Wilderness, for example, jet boats were allowed to run up the Salmon River, airplanes were allowed to continue landing within the wilderness, and a large area was reserved for cobalt mining if the need for cobalt ever became essential. Still, the Wilderness Act has been the envy of many nations, providing inspiration from South Africa to Canada and from India to Costa Rica. It has created protection for animals and plants that can live nowhere else, and it remains a place in the imagination, where all wild things may continue living in a warming climate on an overpopulated planet.

Tom Pomeroy, a longtime supporter of wilderness, provided a more passionate view of unroaded lands in an e-mail:

> I love Wilderness. It's the best and most important resource that Idaho has! It lasts forever and is available for anyone who wants to go there to explore, enjoy, and be grateful that it still exists. I know that compromise is part of the game, but it's so short-sighted to always reduce the issue to what one user group says they need. That's why 95 percent of the continental U.S. is already roaded and gone. The mountain bikers are just another new user group wanting to tear across the landscape so they can say that they "did" it, snap a picture, and then get back home because they're so busy. Many don't want to take the time to enjoy the land on its own terms and think what's best for wildlife, the future, and ever-increasing threats that a rapidly expanding civilization creates.

## The art of war

Whatever you think about Idaho's wilderness, none can say that the debate lacks passion. But since 1964, the human population has grown substantially, forests have burned, the world has grown warmer, and no one dares to dream of a four-day workweek anymore. Recreation for most folks is a lounging trip on a cruise ship in the Caribbean or a daytrip on a mountain bike or a motorized vehicle, riding up and down mountains to gather bragging rights. A few hikers, rafters, kayakers, and horseback riders—seekers of solitude, wildlife, and untrammeled landscapes—seem to value wilderness these days. The greatest value of wild places is their value as a refuge of protected fish and wildlife habitat that only wilderness guarantees.

Simpson is bucking some of his colleagues to get a valuable job done—to protect some wild places in Idaho—and he is accepting compromises in a few beautiful places where some don't think he should. But Simpson is no shrinking violet. He's marching the direction that his heart tells him is the right way. Idaho Conservation League and the Wilderness Society have set course for a national monument. Wilderness area and national monument designations offer both strengths and weaknesses, but the monument is ill defined. Conservationists are at the crossroads, as Simpson moves toward a final conclusion that will resolve the character of the Boulder-White Cloud Mountains. Simpson's supporters are now solid. The primary unanswered question is what Obama will say to Simpson's Boulder-White Clouds Wildernesses.

Simpson advances his new legislation with compromises that recognize the facts on the ground in this conservative state and lead toward completion of a job that began when all the forests still were green, the water ran gin-clear from the mountains, and the sky was not cloudy all day.

*A note from 2021: The Boulder-White Clouds Wilderness was created by law on August 7, 2015, and approved by President Obama, who designated 275,665 acres of the roadless areas and wilderness study areas in Idaho as legally protected wilderness. He designated three areas: the Hemingway-Boulders Wilderness (88,079 acres), the White Clouds Wilderness (90,841 acres), and the Jim McClure-Jerry Peak Wilderness (117,040 acres). These areas are divided by off-road vehicle and mountain bike corridors that had been argued about for more than 30 years. Finally, one of the larger issues in Idaho land politics has been resolved.*

# ELUDING ANTARCTICA

*What if we stayed away from Antarctica and
left the place to the penguins ... and the imagination?
Can we simply leave a place free of human beings?*

I really don't want to see Antarctica. Imagination is more than all of the rock and ice of that southern continent in the West. More than fire and earthquakes, more than oxygen and water, more than blood and guts and low temperatures that freeze spit as it falls, more than Byrd's, Shackleton's, or Amundsen's worthy endeavors, more than a rock star's bizarre desire to be the first to play there. Disallow scientists from further probing and diagnosing the problems in Antarctica. Imagine Antarctica as the place that no one knows.

In this world of Universal Knowledge of the internet, where does wisdom begin or end? I have come to know what Antarctica is from pictures of it: beautiful white and transparent blue ice, ragged mountains, colorful southern auroras and wacky, cute penguins, a few colorful birds, and itty-bitty tiny krill. You know about the krill, right? Imagine quirky little shrimp. They rock and roll where no one can see. Antarctica is a big-rock-and-ice island, surrounded by cold, salty water and chips of ice in the drink that are bigger than any ship, with penguins comically waddling along the rocky places. Seabirds and albatrosses whirl in great numbers and blacken the sky. Enormous whales pass by now-and-again, spouting air and water like grand, living geysers while chasing the itty-bitty krill. Or is it plankton that whales come for? Well, I can read about that on the fabulous World Wide Web. No need to prove reality. Neither narwhals nor unicorns will ever live there nor will any venomous sea snakes churn the waters of Antarctica. Even I know that.

The Ancient Mariner, of Samuel Coleridge fame, lived through a raging hell of vast icebergs, the starving boredom in the doldrums, and defying death riding on a ghostly ship with "water, water everywhere, nor any drop to drink." That is a vision of going to Antarctica that I prefer to live by. It must have been difficult to get there by any means and more difficult to live in for any time. I think that Coleridge had been to Antarctica of the mind and recorded its life most certainly!

*Pictured Left: Adélie penguins on an iceberg in Antarctica.*
PHOTO: JASON-AUCH, WIKIPEDIA

Do whales fall off into the space south of Antarctica? Maybe. But I haven't seen any. I have gained faith in gravity and expect that nothing falls into the abyss of sky. That's the scientific mind at work. That's my reality. But that collective mind hasn't done much to protect our planet. (Or does this planet even need our protection?) I know that we have affected all the world with our growing populations and technology: from developing weapons with our many brilliant theories (lots of oddball weapons: arrows, slings, spears, bullets, fire, lasers, atomic and hydrogen bombs, ad nauseam have been the result) protecting us from people who don't share our opinions. Destroying societies, plant and animal communities. Protecting us from all of the uncertainties, all of the irrational things in life as they are understood. From the flat world. From darkness. From the plague. From cancer. From death. From aging. From a cult of others: Russians, Chinese, Tibetans, Polynesians, the Religious, or more current villains, from the white and the black races. It is as if understanding will give us knowledge and knowledge will convey safety. Isn't that right? But where is the dividing line between survival and domination?

We have met the indomitable opponent of our own ambition. To eat, drink, and procreate in vast comfort are our birthrights. Right? Why would any one of us want to reduce our standard of living? And so we progress to the edge of the lemmings' cliff knowing that we will fall and fail. Is it too late to push back? We charm ourselves into believing it is not too late for oil and food and medicines to save humanity. But we only live a day before we die. And then what have we left? Today only 7.8 billion people cover the world with their great gifts of humanity.

Could we simply leave Antarctica alone for a change? I mean really. To have peace where no human beings see, hike on, play concerts for the thrill of it, or fly over? Of course there are already photographs, but they open our imagination more than describe the icy continent. Our survival could depend upon our creativity and using our imaginations.

I hope krill live long and prosper in the Antarctic seawater, in warmth below the icebergs, and in the ecstasy of the warming waters of Antarctica. Let the penguins waddle in peace. Do we need to deal with the fact that their habitat, and ours, is diminishing? Yes, but not

particularly in Antarctica. We've already seen that even Antarctica has been damaged by our exploits. Food will be less, people will be more, water will be higher, storms bigger, as many catastrophes swirl. As we measure the disaster. All I ask is to just leave Antarctica alone. As alone as possible. Maybe, like Atlantis, it will sink beneath the sea. However, I need a place to hold my dreams in my time on this bloody, beautiful planet.

There are plenty of facts showing that Antarctica is changing rapidly and that we're not doing a damn thing about it. Nothing, anyway, that is likely to stop the world from warming. We probe it and pick at it and define the loss, like lepers in the time before antibiotics. We can all take a look at ice coring and see what has happened before we came to power or look at the rising tide and $CO_2$ levels. What do we do but say beyond "doggone it?" I've heard the message chimed out to the world: the world is warming. And cooking slowly.

So what? So we may go back to the Ice Age of yesterday. So what? What is the new "antibiotic?" "We need a new drug," to quote Huey Lewis, and it may cure us for a while. We could use some new respect for this limited planet.

*The blue ice covering Lake Fryxell, in the Transantarctic Mountains of Antarctica.*

Scientists, using the scientific method, make systematic observations, measurements, and define experiments. We form and test our hypotheses before making brash proclamations. Our knowledge is slow moving, unimpeachable, and essential. We have discovered the underlying factors of life, nucleic acid by nucleic acid. We've unlocked the secrets of atomic structure. And what has that accomplished, other than knowing that we could blow ourselves up? Well, among other things we may be able to reconstruct the life force of the Tyrannosaurus Rex or the passenger pigeon, which, of course, we may well have exterminated, and save other endangered species by analyzing their genetic components. We could extend our lives to, well, perhaps, forever. And make more money to give us a better life, a happier life, a richer life! But when one gains, another loses. Or as poet Alexander Pope wrote more succinctly, we are "Created half to rise and half to fall; Great lord of all things, yet a prey to all." Do we want to be that forever?

*The sinking of Sir Ernest Shackleton's ship* Endurance *in Antarctica, November 1915.*

What does any of this have to do with leaving Antarctica alone? I suppose not much. But my Antarctica, to the west of west, allows mysteries to remain. I will imagine that continent of ice. It is a place, just like all other places, that is—today—being made less mysterious. Is more known of Antarctica today than yesterday? Probably. But why, what has been gained by this expanding knowledge of ours? Interesting stuff, I suppose.

I want to know that Shackleton didn't make it to the South Pole, that it was unattainable, that human ambition has its limits. Struggling serves its purpose for humanity but I don't want to know exactly what happened to him. That he survived an Odyssean journey is plenty. Must we know everything? Can we? Failing is our greatest victory; it is the one thing that we cannot fully achieve until the moment when we fail decisively, enormously, and finally. We all fail. We all leave our home.

This is the beauty of Antarctica: it is futile, basically useless to me and to you. Sure there are plenty of beauties in Antarctica: the vicious cold, tall mountains, deep crevasses, and all of that. But this is the place where, if you choose to go, you risk only death and the unknowable. If I go, I must go alone—not with a crew of others to support me—and if a small thing goes wrong, I will not return: no heroic flights, no resupplying, no support groups. It should be a place where the world remains flat with our fear of falling off into oblivion. Or we just freeze. And die alone.

For me, Antarctica embodies the greatest mystery, the only reality that I know that I know. Antarctica is the place where all my dreams might come true! It is better than the vacuum of outer space where nothing lives. Tread carefully on this forbidden continent and don't bother to record its decline. Know that it is receding and there will never be another left like it. Isn't it enough to let it be and tell tall tales, Viking tales, tales of the southern aurora in Antarctica? Perhaps you might come back from Antarctica, assuming that you go in your mind, as wise as the Mariner realizing that "He prayeth well who loveth well; both man and bird and beast. He prayest best who loveth best; All things both great and small." We should love Antarctica by letting her be herself. Or itself. Maybe it is in my mind. Out West, surviving.

# SACRED DIRT

A deep, clear pool invited two of us to dive into the water and swim. We were hot and sweaty from hiking and of course we took that invitation to take a dip and splash one another. I crawled out dripping and cooler and lay on a rosy sandstone slab beside the pool in the shade of a stately cottonwood tree and fell asleep beside my lover. I found it a simple and elegant place to lie, out of the hot midday sun, away from motorized vehicles, away from the hustle-bustle of life, with my gal. That was in 1986. The pool was smaller when I went there a few years later and that gal was long gone. Last year the broad-leaved tree that shaded the slab in afternoons, had fallen. It was a beauty with stout limbs, smaller branches, and wildly rustling leaves. Now the pool collected sediment; a stream ran through it and dissipated in a rock drainage. It is no longer a pool but a drying tributary of Arch Canyon Creek. It had changed, but this place, in the midst of Arch Canyon, near Blanding, Utah, still looked pure and undisturbed.

I suppose that I, too, had changed over those years. Please allow me to explain, but you mustn't hold me to a linear timeline: mine is a wandering tale covering 35 years of fevers and, I hope, lucid tellings, stitched together with sinew and hope.

When I attended a meeting at Bluff, Utah, in June 2016, Secretary of Interior Sally Jewell and key others in the U.S. Interior and Agriculture Departments were there to listen to the opinions of people who came from around the state to this tiny, historic town. Its history included a well-known fort that was an outpost for Mormon colonizers. The meeting with Jewell, as the listener for what became President Obama's Bears Ears National Monument, which included Arch Canyon, was filled with the anger and opinions of nearly 2,000 people milling around the meeting house. Here are a few comments spoken by Native Americans:

> Rebecca Benally, a former County Commissioner from San Juan County, asked the panel, "Why do we need 1.9 million acres of the National Monument? Why do we need another federal agency to protect our land at all?" The mountains have been fine up to this point, she said.

*Pictured Left: Hiking up Arch Canyon where water can always be found.*

Octavia Seowtewa, a respected medicine man in the Zuni Tribe, said: "We need the protection of the land, animals, and archeology."

Malcom Lehi, Ute Mountain Tribal Commissioner, added, "We need to protect the sacred qualities in the land, the talking of the wind in the woods and the dirt."

Jonah Yellowman, a Navajo spiritual leader, asked this question: "What is your trail? Who can catch the hummingbird in your hand? The hummingbird led me to something beautiful. It was spiritual guidance, animals, and preserving the land. We learn from it. Our prayers have led us all in this endeavor."

I sat for many hours listening to the testimony and eventually my mind wandered. I remembered watching a monarch butterfly with a broken wing that had come to live beside my camp midway through Arch Canyon. It lit upon a tall sagebrush and could go nowhere else in this world. It could fly a little, but neither high nor far. This monarch, with stark black lines crossing its salmon-colored wings, had to be content with its limitations, its impaired but astonishing beauty in this small paradise within the sacred dirt of Arch Canyon.

△△△

In 1988, jeeps headed up Arch Canyon by twos and threes until there were 25 of them. Environmentalists and jeepers traded insults and obscene gestures at the base of the canyon where jeeps were set to run on their special route. All of the environmental staff got quoted in the Salt Lake City press, setting off petty fireworks that lasted for years of discontent. Scott Groene and I, both in what William Shakespeare might have called our "salad days, green in judgment, cold in blood," planned to follow the jeeps up Arch Canyon, taking photos and engaging the drivers in "what-the-hell-are-you-doing-here" conversations at every opportunity. Scott and I felt that we would win this battle by the divine power of being pissed off. And, of course, we were simply correct. Scott was an advocate, a lawyer, for the Navajo and lived in a hogan down by Bluff, and I worked for the Wilderness Society as its Utah representative in Salt Lake City.

We wanted Arch Canyon to be Wilderness, with a capital W, not a mangled motorized speedway. The jeepers wanted to have some fun and prove their ability to ride anywhere. Which they did on that day. That seemed much too much to Scott and me. We took pictures of one jeep stuck in deep mud with free-spinning wheels throwing mud every which-way as the vehicles climbed up improbable stream banks and made one helluva mess of this lovely creek, jeopardizing, it seemed to me, wildlife, fish, cliff dwellings, ruins, other artifacts, and insulting the superb scenery in Arch Canyon.

Today, in 2021, the Jeep Jamboree has been in business for more than 30 years and every year jeeps head up Arch Canyon with typical Mormon enthusiasm and goodness. The Southern Utah Wilderness Alliance (SUWA) and Groene, who is now SUWA's executive director, had sought to get Arch Canyon protected from the vehicles, but two things thwarted them. First, the way up Arch Canyon had long been declared a legal Right of Way, which allowed access to motorized vehicles and, second, SUWA's legal petition demanding closure of Arch Canyon to protect the archeological, biological, and wilderness values in the canyon. A response to SUWA's petition, written by the Bureau of Land Management's (BLM's) Monticello Field Office

*Stirring up water and politics.*

archeologist, Donald Simonis, identified 38 significant cultural sites within 100 feet of the trail running up Arch Canyon. That included cliff dwellings, petroglyphs, granaries, a very rare great kiva, and the three-story ruins at the base of Arch Canyon.

SUWA's petition, good as it was, failed to win the case in federal court to eliminate jeep traffic. However, the BLM's response forced the jeeps, and now the more modern bug-eyed dune buggies that climb like daddy-longlegs spiders, to follow a particular route and to protect all of the identified cultural values. It was a painful compromise.

Keep in mind that parts of that road are washed out virtually every year with flood water, often making the road impossible to define. At the base of the canyon, jeep trails run haywire looking for that legal Right of Way until they get upstream where the canyon forces them into a narrow passage. The machines continue to take the trip up Arch Canyon, but at the end of the nine-mile route they must halt. There they are stopped cold by strict management of the U.S. Forest Service (USFS) in this Inventoried Roadless Area.

△△△

Arch Canyon is divided in land management between the BLM and the USFS, with the BLM managing the lower nine miles, where most of the cultural values are located, and the USFS managing the upper part, beyond where the canyons split like a hand stretching out. The USFS portion of Arch Canyon includes Arch, Texas, and Butts canyons, and it has never been designated as a Wilderness, in the legal sense. It probably never will. Only diminishingly few hikers who endure nine miles of what many see as obnoxious motor sounds and rowdy behavior would ever see the three higher, deeper, more colorful, and profound canyons or any of the many cultural sites on the way up. But, this circumstance has provided an entirely wild feeling in the upper canyons. It has brought silence to that land. In the years that I've been hiking Arch Canyon—often every year—I have seen other non-motorized hikers beyond the USFS boundary exactly twice. In Butts Canyon, my favorite, I have never seen another human soul.

I had a near-death stroke 20 years ago in Craters of the Moon National Monument and Preserve in Idaho. I was carried out in a helicopter to the town of Pocatello where I began a lengthy recovery process. Part of that process included hiking again in Arch Canyon, with its wide stone arches, cinnamon colored thousand-foot walls, and magnificent cliff dwellings. Most important to me as I recovered is that much of Arch is a canyon-complex of silence, rock, aloneness, and animals. The world of upper Arch Canyon is the place in Cedar Mesa that filled me with a renewed sense of wonder, something I had lost in having a nearly unbearable stroke. I saw wildlife—deer, red-tailed hawks, a prairie falcon, coyotes, butterflies, one rattlesnake (in all those years it was only one), dozens of collared and side-blotched lizards, an Abert's squirrel (they're curious, shaggy-eared little buggers!), ringtails, nighthawks, and hummingbirds. I heard dramatic and inspirational descending glissandos of canyon wrens which exuded their immense joy at being in this canyon. Trees thrived in the shade of canyon walls: pinyon pines, juniper, Douglas fir, and Ponderosa pines among them.

When Scott Groene and I walked up the canyon chasing motorized vehicles many years ago, their grinding noises so inappropriate to us, the last thing I expected to see were Ponderosa pines in the bottom of this desert canyon. On later trips up Arch Canyon, bear tracks led me into deeper wilderness canyons and I was charmed by the four waterfalls in Butts Canyon. When water was hard to find, there were springs. When deluge came, there were alcoves. When my mind dimmed, the canyon brought inspiration. The creek ran year-round and magic owned the canyons.

△△△

Pepper, my knee-high Catahoula puppy, and I reached Arch Canyon in 2019, a week after a flash flood washed through Arch Canyon. The water had receded but the creek remained cloudy, and we would have to cross Arch Canyon Creek 52 times to get up the creek to the arches. My challenge was to get Pepper to cross the creek at all because she was afraid of water. The water was muddy, roughly 30 feet wide in places, and we couldn't see more than two inches into it. I crossed it once and stood on the opposite bank calling her. She looked at me as if I was too stupid to understand. "Come on, Pepper! Come on, girl!" She was not coming. No way.

She looked up and down the creek. Nowhere was she promised an easy ford. She whined and looked frantic, as if to say "Come on friend. This is freaking silly. I don't want to drown!" I stood there and continued to call. "Come on. Come on, Pepper!" Finally, she took a leap of faith and went clomping through the water, swimming and thrump, thrump, thrumping with her paws, her little head barely staying up. She looked desperate but finally she climbed out on my side of the creek, clearly delighted with herself and apparently happy to have survived. She shook on me as some kind of sign of her

*This monarch butterfly was marooned in Arch Canyon; not a bad place in which to be stuck.*

failing respect, and we went onward. Another 51 crossings to go. Each crossing became progressively easier for her to conquer and by the end of day she was a champion creek-crosser.

Pepper and I camped above the boundary of the USFS land because we found that the best campsite in Arch Canyon was already inhabited. But from our site we could see the first major arch, Angel Arch. In certain light this arch jumps out at you. Other times it hides in flat lighting. Regardless, on the next morning I saw a group of four hikers marching up beside my camp and we chatted a bit. They were planning to head up to Angel Arch with their clinking gear as I was packing up to go farther up the canyon to look at Keystone Arch and hike in Butts Canyon with my daypack.

When I returned, I hoped to have a conversation with these men and ask how the climb was. Climbing on sandstone sounded very dicey to me but I was surprised to find their campsite deserted. It pleased me enormously to inherit their campsite, but as I walked around their camp I saw that they had left many things of value. That led me to believe they had left in a hurry: shoes, a nice pair of short pants, socks, and a beautiful t-shirt. They didn't simply leave; they must've run, cleared out, bailed, leaving valuable clothes and other odd remnants. But, my God, who climbs on crumbly sandstone? Or on a sublime arch?

Sand ran through the men's hands on a failed pitch, as one of them fell, breaking his arm and yelling at his pain as the others scurried to pick him up. I never found out what actually happened to them, but I imagine they had a long bumpy, splashy, painfully long way out on their ATV ride toward Blanding. My imagination came from my unexpected stroke out in the wild land of Idaho: I imagined pain radiating from the wounded man's arm and his cringing with every one of those 52 crossings and hundreds of wheel-bouncing bumps. However, my fate was better this time: I inherited their good campsite and some well-fitting, handsome short pants.

△△△

When I was working for the Wilderness Society in the 1980s as the Utah representative, I heard about a monument proclamation that was written specifically for Arch Canyon for President Franklin D. Roosevelt to proclaim. Keep in mind that the president has almost unlimited power to create a national monument. Many years afterward I looked in a variety of Utah libraries and eventually talked with a friend and teacher in Idaho, John Freemuth. He knew about such things, had earned his Ph.D., and was concerned with the history of public lands management in the West. I offered him my evidence about Arch Canyon and we talked about the original Escalante Proclamation of 4 million acres in the time of way-back-when. We talked about Ed Abbey and others who had done their best to protect this enormous landscape. We talked about the Grand Staircase-Escalante National Monument that was protected and had whipped a coal mine. I told him I was looking for something smaller, specifically about Arch Canyon. He offered skepticism at first, but we crafted a couple of questions that would go to the archives in the National Park Service (NPS) and then he sent the request to his friend, then-director of the NPS.

Freemuth called me in a month and said, "Mike, you'll have to look at what we found. I think you'll like it." He laughed in a pleasant way. That was Freemuth—he taunted. But he taunts no more—last year he died swiftly of a heart attack. But what he found was a proclamation written by NPS officials offered under the signature of former Secretary of Interior Harold Ickes. Arch Canyon was proposed as a national monument in late 1939, and that proclamation had apparently lingered on the desk of President Franklin Roosevelt. The 53,100-acre area never got further discussion, apparently because World War II had begun and public attention obviously looked elsewhere to the collapsing Europe and then to Pearl Harbor. Or perhaps the lobbying of anti—national monument naysayers triumphed. Regardless, the proclamation stated the following:

> Arch Canyon is an area of high mesas and deep canyons. The precipitous cliffs, natural arches and other odd erosional forms, which are features of the area, have been carved in the gray and buff Cedar Mesa Sandstone of Permian age. The light colored walls of the canyon contrast vividly with the plant covered uplands eroded from the Organ Rock beds of De Chelly sandstone and the maroon strata of the Moenkopi formation.

> Erosion is the predominant geologic process illustrated within this monument. It has produced cliffs from 1,000 to 1,500 feet high as well as the arches from which the canyon derives its name.... Three of the most spectacular ones have been named: Angel Arch, Cathedral Arch, and Keystone Arch. Cathedral Arch is a towering rock mass suggestive of a flying buttress supporting the walls of a cathedral. Keystone Arch is an isolated mass of cross-bedded sandstone pierced by an angular opening the ragged edges of which resemble projecting segments of the primitive arch.

Support had gained for the monument as early as 1937 and in a memorandum to NPS policy maker Herbert Maier, NPS geologist Charles Gould wrote:

> From the standpoint of geology the valley resembles Zion National Park. It is a region of high mesas, deep canyons and cliffs.... In Arch Canyon, according to Mr. Johnson [Zeke Johnson, former custodian of Natural Bridges National

*Angel Arch in Arch Canyon.*

Monument] there is heavy timber, chiefly pine, spruce, fir and allied species. Many springs occur. The cliffs are 1,000 to 2,000 feet in height. Many prehistoric dwellings are found, so that from the standpoint of geology, wildlife and archeology, Arch Canyon would appear to have possibilities.

△△△

Tribal governments in this region (Uinta and Ouray Ute, Navajo, Hopi, Ute Mountain Ute, and the Zuni) formed the Bears Ears Intertribal Coalition to retain their stolen world along with its spiritual values. Environmental groups, in another coalition, which included the Sierra Club, the Wilderness Society, and SUWA among them, sought to protect Wilderness areas and cultural sites on the federal Bears Ears land. Both coalitions communicated closely beginning in 2010 and, along with key attorneys, they formed an important bond to define a strong national monument. Virtually all of these people knew the shakers-and-movers in the Obama administration and the agency staff for the BLM, USFS, and NPS that managed public lands in Utah. Each group sought and found foundations to fund their efforts. The Tribes recommended protection of 1.9 million acres of

Cedar Mesa, which they named the Bears Ears National Monument, and submitted their proposal to President Obama in October 2015.

In December 2016, six months after the public meeting I attended in Bluff, President Obama made a proclamation and in it he identified the 1.35-million-acre Bears Ears National Monument. That enraged the Utah Delegation in Washington, D.C., but it could give the Tribes an important role in managing and, potentially in controlling, the new monument in San Juan County, Utah. The Tribes made a point in their proposal, insisting on collaborative management of the land. That would allow them to work with the land managers on an equal basis, government to government, and to be recognized for what the Tribes represented in the Bears Ears National Monument.

However, and everything in this story is broken by "However," like the word in a broken treaty, the Bears Ears National Monument was short lived when President Trump won America's leadership in 2016, surprising all the world. In 2017, President Trump listened to the Utah Delegation claim they had done everything they could to offer a unique solution to the Cedar Mesa conflicts and that the wide group of organizations had rejected that negotiated offer in favor of an inflated Bears Ears National Monument. President Trump took the Utah politicians at their word and reduced Obama's monument by nearly 85 percent, replacing it with a pair of national monuments: *Shash Ja'a* at 129,980 acres and Indian Creek at 71,896 acres. Arch Canyon was protected in both Obama's and Trump's proclamations, but Trump allowed oil and gas extraction and mining in what was Obama's more protective 1.35-million-acre monument.

*Shash Ja'a*, the Navajo words for the Bears Ears, protects Arch Canyon in its entirety along with Comb Ridge, the Bears Ears geologic site, Moon House and Doll House Ruins, and many other sacred sites. But it failed to protect other places like Grand Gulch, Slickhorn Canyon, Fish and Owl Canyons, and failed to extinguish uranium claims or protect the land from oil and gas drilling. Moreover, in November 2020 voters selected Native American leaders, Kenneth Maryboy and Willie Grayeyes, to the San Juan Commission, which has authority over management of the Bears Ears region. That wasn't what conservatives in San Juan County expected or hoped for as both Maryboy and Grayeyes are ardent supporters of the original Bears Ears National Monument. However, supporters of the Bears Ears National Monument had lost 85 percent of the land in the monument sweepstakes process, and that stung. But now there is momentum for protecting the whole Bears Ears National Monument and the Tribes have the ear of the new Interior Secretary, Deb Haaland, a Native American chosen by President Biden.

Let me give Arch Canyon the credit for what it is and why it was given recognition from President Trump.

Arch Canyon is a key to biological diversity in the Cedar Mesa region because it is sizeable, it abuts the large Dark Canyon Wilderness Area, is surrounded by major undeveloped regions (like White Canyon and its tributaries, Hammond Canyon, Mule Canyon, and Natural Bridges National Monument), has significant elevation variation (from 4,900 to 8,000 feet), has substantial vegetative diversity (from sagebrush to Ponderosa pines), includes lots of wildlife, riparian areas, cultural values, and, more than any other single virtue, it has year-round running water. According to a 2005 fish survey by the Utah Division of Wildlife Resources, there were bluehead suckers, mountain suckers, speckled dace, and fathead minnow in Arch Canyon Creek. That's not terribly spectacular, but the fish were there, proving that the drainage had always flowed water. In late summer, when the canyons all around Arch Canyon are dry, many animals come into Arch Canyon Creek to drink. I've seen bear tracks every year late in the season, and bears are very rare in the canyons of Southern Utah.

*Water flowing toward a fall in Butts Canyon.*

Every time I go to Arch Canyon I take the hike up Butts Canyon, a tributary to Arch, to follow bear tracks into this sublime gulch. It is an easy hike without a trail as the stream crosses a meadow of burned timber and winds up a sinuous route to where the canyon narrows. Three times in different years I've seen animals in Butts Canyon: coyotes, deer, hawks, squirrels, and tracks of bears. There are hanging gardens and many pour-offs that protect brilliant scarlet penstemon and yellow monkeyflowers. The narrow stream that wanders through this canyon falls off four cliffs on its way down. Some years I've taken a shower here under my choice of waterfalls, and when it's way too cold I've simply listened to the crash of water on rock as it swirls off the cliff into bright sunlight. The view from the first waterfall is the most memorable sight of Arch Canyon, framed by canyon walls and Ponderosa pines. It is not possible to enhance this slice of perfection, and it has done my head many miracles.

△△△

Tribes and environmental groups expressed their unanimous opposition to Trump's monument for being too small, and several groups filed overlapping lawsuits against the change. One claim stated that Trump had never been given specific authority to reduce the monument and his actions were therefore illegal. The Antiquities Act also requires that the president proclaim any monument included as "the smallest area compatible with the proper care and management of the objects to be protected." The specific wording of the Obama proclamation defined the 1.35 million acres as the smallest monument that could protect the thousands of cultural objects. The Trump proclamation asserted that the *Shash Ja'a* and Indian Creek National Monuments defined the smallest monument needed to protect the crucial and adored objects. The 1906 Antiquities Act, like the Mining Law of 1872, is a law that never anticipated the modern world; it made essential generalities that were equal to the date when the law was enacted. How would they be interpreted in today's world? How many objects needed protection? How much land should be included? How much was a political call in today's world?

Nobody knows. Ask the Supreme Court. Times have changed and many laws have evolved to protect significant objects that I believe required preservation. Trump cited some of the more recent laws, such as the Endangered Species Act, the Archeological Resources Protection Act, the Federal Lands Policy Management Act, the Wilderness Act, and other laws, in saying that many of the objects are already protected outside of the national monument. That was part of Trump's reason for shrinking national monuments, but at the same time he sought reduction of the compass of the other laws that would protect the values of the national monuments.

Several cases exist in which presidents, other than Trump, had diminished the size of a national monument by as much as

89 percent. In 1915 President Wilson cut 313,280 acres from the 639,200-acre Mount Olympus National Monument in Washington State. It appears that Trump is not alone in expressing his wishes, and none of the proclamations have been overturned. Now with the recently elected Democratic majority in Congress, the fortune of the Tribes and environmentalists has changed. Supporters of the larger Bears Ears National Monument have challenged the smaller *Shash Ja'a* and Indian Creek National Monuments but have suggested that they may drop their challenge with Biden at the helm.

The Bears Ears National Monument was indeed re-proclaimed with the original 2016 boundaries atop the Trump national monument by President Biden in 2021. That action, predictably, enraged the Utah Delegation and Utah's Governor. Utah's politicians issued a strong statement stating that the controversy over boundaries of the monument should be resolved by a collaboration and consensus effort that would decisively resolve the contested issues. In the absence of that effort they claimed that a lawsuit may follow and opined that this new lawsuit will likely have to be resolved by the Supreme Court because of all the back-and-forth Antiquities Act actions that have occurred for more than 25 years in Utah. Alternatively, the monument definition could be enshrined in law by passing legislation about the monument. That is what legislation has done in the Craters of the Moon National Monument and Preserve in Idaho and in the legal designation of the National Petroleum Reserve in Alaska.

Fortunately, Arch Canyon, as part of the *Shash Ja'a* and Bears Ears National Monuments, is likely to win either way the Supreme Court decides on the two conflicting national monument plans because both Presidents Obama and Trump, and now Biden, have aimed to protect this rather obscure canyon in its entirety. I believe that it is because of the 1939 documentation of the original proposed proclamation for Arch Canyon that encouraged Trump to proclaim *Shash Ja'a* as a wholly defensible national monument.

△△△

I am not religious, but I can feel the world when it calls out to me. I climbed up to a cliff dwelling that I had walked past and seen a dozen times. It is known by some as the Jailhouse Ruin in Arch Canyon. I climbed alone up a steep incline toward a broken rimrock and ran into two or three dead-end routes before finding one that I might slip through to get up to the ruin. I climbed between two broken rocks, shimmied up beside a large juniper, and crawled up to an exposed stretch of steeply tilted sandstone. I rounded a short hill that increased in pitch as I went up. It was barely doable for me, but I got to the top and traversed to a point below the Jailhouse Ruin where I could look up into it. The ruin was well named. It looked like a jail room with a series of vertical sticks blocking the window. For years, I wanted to see what was inside that cell and now I sat right outside the ruin, looking up into it from 100 feet below. It was now easily accessible.

Something happened. It was like the twang of a breaking harp string in the silence of Anton Chekov's play *The Cherry Orchard* which speaks of a warning or an abrupt change in invisible power. It is the tomahawk thrown that sticks beside your head—thwang—a dramatic warning! I felt a power, some *éminence grise*, insisting that I not go an inch closer. It was a curious thing, like a cold breeze on the nape of my neck in mid-summer. I suspect that it was the same

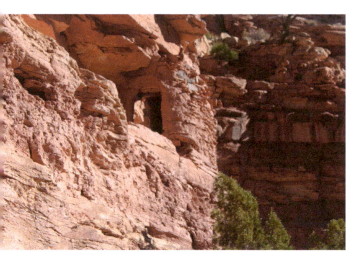

One of many Anasazi ruins in Arch Canyon.

warning that the climbers ignored in climbing on the arch. I looked for a long time—noticing that there were two rooms in the ruin—and got up to enter into it. But then I felt that this place suddenly had become dangerous. I stopped, oddly paralyzed, and looked around for the jailhouse guardian shaking skeleton keys. There was no such person.

I turned back and headed downhill. I looked back into the ruin for another half-minute from farther below, out of some curiosity and a desire to remember the place as I left it. I had no need to enter that dwelling after making the hard climb up to it. None. I tell you that with some embarrassment. And certainty. I cannot tell you why, but a gut feeling convinced me not to enter this ancient dwelling. Jailhouse Ruin felt as if it were the realm of past sprits that had nothing to do with me. But might, if I wasn't careful. I knew the price of a minor mistake from my experience in Craters of the Moon and I didn't want to risk another stroke in judgment. There seems no time limit to this curse or to the blessing I had received. But there was something. I climbed safely down.

The Arch Canyon Ruins at the base of the canyon elicited an entirely different response from me: sorrow and guilt. You can feel the sorrow of the people who lived here who left their home and never returned. These were the finest dwellings in Cedar Mesa once upon a time. Of course, they could be rebuilt with the stones that lie beside the ruins and might bring back the glory of their unknown past. But look at the BLM sign that announces the Arch Canyon Ruin. It is old. The worn-out fence around the ruin is broken down, and the soil beside that sign mostly grows cheatgrass. The place feels abandoned. It is abandoned. What caused the three-story buildings to topple is anyone's guess. It must've been a noble site to live in, but now it has become horribly and shockingly neglected. It could become a proud site like those in Grand Gulch which have been rebuilt, cared for, and loved. But maybe, just maybe, sorrow is the right feeling to have for the Arch Canyon Ruins. That is another form of spiritual magic: the power of departing, never to return. A symbol of death and the destruction of a culture.

Peace and contentment, however, are what I've felt in most of Arch Canyon. I no longer chase jeeps. I recognize that the smoothness in my rough-and-tumbled, stroke-damaged mind is a gift. I've come to a truce with the motorized crowd after 30 years of hating them. I have a growing love for this creek and the canyon's rugged elegance, respect for the opinions of environmental advocates and Native Americans, a sense of the power in the untouchable and spiritual world, a taste for the infinite, and a reminder to live my life simply, to touch the land whenever I can. All of these are gifts from hiking Arch Canyon. And from my stroke. By and by, the whole of Arch Canyon will get what it needs in the arena of human wants, and I know that its beauty and its wildlife will survive if we want it to. I know that I do. But how will the broader deserving landscapes be preserved as our human population continues to grow? How does a Monarch butterfly survive with its wings trimmed to the nub? These are koans I am still working to resolve.

# MEDITATION ON THE DEATH OF TWO WOMEN

W hen lava flowed into the valley of Craters of the Moon 2,000 years ago, limber pines burst into flames. Only molds of trees stood when the rock cooled and solidified as trees were incinerated. Were you lured by this magic, by these sirens in stone? You walked into a vast maze of desert rock, sharp, irregular, and raven black. With no path leading out. Dehydration came, breath by breath, and you lost your way in this trailless wilderness. There can be no exit if the way in is lost! Blistering in sunshine, freezing at night; confusion came like a blink, death like a holy vision.

Every time I come into this black wilderness, I, too, flirt with immortality.

# FRENCH CREEK: LOST IN A LOST DRAINAGE

I n 1995, Rocky Barker, a writer for the *Idaho Statesman*, and I were up in the air looking over French Creek in Central Idaho after the major Blackwell and Corral fires burned through the drainage the year before. I assumed that the vee of the drainage hadn't burned, because I had hiked the upper part of French Creek after the 1994 fires and saw that it was burned in a typical mosaic pattern: here charcoal, there green trees, and in riparian areas the damage was spotty. On the airplane flight, I was surprised that the entire lower portion of French Creek was burned like it had been set on fire with a welding torch. It was a high-intensity fire area, and much of the upper portion was scorched as well.

From the air, many snags looked like burnt matchsticks in what was once my favorite forest in Idaho. I wonder what happened to all of the wildlife in that drainage. I guess they ran or flew away. Rocky gave me a "sorry, man" sort of hang-dog look, and I don't even remember what he wrote for the *Statesman*. A bleak story of a lost drainage is what I expected, but I know he had a more complicated view of fire, having experienced the Yellowstone fires years before. My view is that every forest burns, and every forest will recover in time.

Long before the fires, in the 1980s, logging in French Creek was planned by the Forest Service. And later, the watershed was surveyed at least twice for road building. In 1995, Congress, including Idaho Senator Larry Craig, passed legislation suspending preparation of an environmental analysis for the French Creek roadless area immediately after the fires. That made cutting the trees there easier and made it impossible to challenge with a legal appeal. I figured that the environment would be the longtime loser, with roads and clearcuts covering what had been a wild landscape until then. The French Creek timber sales, when they were suspended from the NEPA (National Environmental Policy Act) rules, ended up on the fastest track possible at the time I asked Rocky to fly over French Creek with me. I assumed that the press would be a powerful voice for protection.

*Pictured Left: Little French Creek flowing through a meadow.*

As we flew, the landscape below us looked bleak, with all of the timber burned except the big Ponderosa pines in the upper drainage. Those trees had to be the real target of the French Creek salvage timber sale. "Pumpkins," as the big Ponderosa pines were termed by foresters, were surely the high-money logs that the timber industry coveted. These big pines have a rich ochre color in their bark and they exude a sweet vanilla smell throughout the forest. The trees looked elegant standing in the otherwise blackened forest. They survived the fire just as you might suspect from thick-barked pines. Now they would be offered at bargain prices at a salvage timber sale. But is a salvage timber sale worse than a large burn? I had an opinion about that.

I developed a response to the logging plan with key supporters to oppose the post-fire French Creek timber sales, after previous plans had twice been defeated. Both of those times, appeals had delayed the logging, but in all honesty, the landscape would be so hard to log that the timber sales received no competitive bids. This time, though, it might be easier to log because of the fires, and I had no opportunity to write an appeal to protect the values of the land and wildlife. There is a great deal of elevation loss from Black Tip Mountain in the headwaters of French Creek to the Salmon River where it culminates, and thus the land supports a wide variety of animals and plants. But this landscape would simply be cremated after a big fire, roadbuilding, and logging; its essence would be forever altered.

I took a New Meadows District ranger to see the Ponderosa pines that were slated for logging and tried to convince her that the trees had not grown to the point where they had "culminated," a forestry term used for trees that have begun to slow down their growth and were therefore ready to cut. It was a tough point to make, but by-and-by and for whatever reasons, these timber sales were not approved by the Forest Service. French Creek would remain the pristine place it had been for millennia.

That was more than 20 years ago. And that is how the environment is protected in Idaho these days: by plodding, step-by-step, and maybe you get a break. French Creek got many breaks and now seems to be threatened only by motorcycles and mountain bikes. That is no threat at all, though, by comparison to when French

Creek was quartered and drawn by surveyors and survived thrice, by hook and by crook.

In 2018, it would be time for me to hike once again along French Creek to fish, enjoy the scenery, and watch wildlife in solitude. I wanted to hike my long-forgotten friend and see what time had done with the drainage.

I asked three people to hike with me, but all were busy on the Fourth of July weekend I planned to hike down Little French Creek and then cross over and hike up main French Creek. So I hiked alone. The trip would be 30 miles, and I would end up where I began, at Fisher Creek Saddle. This was a neat circle, except that I'd never hiked the point from Black Tip Mountain to Fisher Creek Saddle. It looked a little dicey on the topo map, but I'd negotiate it if need be. Maybe I would.

The view from Fisher Creek Saddle was superb as I looked out to the headwaters of Little French Creek. Beyond that were Center Ridge and the larger French Creek proper. Dropping down a ways from Fisher Creek Saddle, I could look up at the severe cirque of 8,700-foot Bruin Mountain, at several other carved-out mountains beside it, and at the valley cascading down from the saddle. Shooting star flowers and avalanche lilies told me that snow had left this point relatively recently, maybe two weeks prior to my trip. These, my favorite flowers, were everywhere, along with elk and deer tracks. A decent trail headed south and precipitously downhill. Within half a mile, I found trickling water and a large cougar track. There the trail became hard to follow. Buckbrush up to my armpits was the main feature between occasional "trailettes."

A trailette, in my book, is one of those bits of trail that keep you hoping that it will lead to somewhere useful but that die off after about 100 yards in a tangle of brush, a stack of fallen trees, or, typically, at an impasse: a cliff, river, marsh, meadow, or a nearly passible descent that offers a temptation to at least try that route. Someone had cleared intermittent parts of the trail for a mile or so, but it seemed that the trailmaker soon became discouraged at finishing the job. Perhaps the person dissolved or was eaten; I couldn't say with any accuracy. However, I began to see regular cougar tracks ahead of mine and several piles of bear feces that

*Shooting stars!*

could have discouraged that intrepid trailblazer—or been parts of the last remains of him or her. Regardless, there was not a hint of a trail for the next eight or nine miles of the downstream route. The route was crisscrossed with burned and fallen trees, sometimes laid in two, three, or four levels against my progress. I could see why no one wanted to get to Little French Creek, but that, of course, was its main charm. It was remote and untraveled by anyone but a driven fool. For wildlife, it was paradise.

I can hear you asking, "Why didn't you walk through the seven miles of meadow along Little French? They are beautiful and look much easier to negotiate." Wrong-o, my friend! I tried it, but the meadowland in the Little French Creek drainage is difficult to travel without a trail. The first problem is that the magnificent, hip-deep grasses that sway most entrancingly, hide many fallen trees and invisible, but deep, rivulets. That's not such a vast problem unless you're crossing several miles of meadow with trees like big-assed anacondas occurring at odd intervals of roughly six feet. These snakes will catch your shoelaces, sending you headlong into the grass. The invisible creeks made me stumble, and with my 40-pound pack, I was thrown ass-over-teakettle more than a few times, winding up face-first into quagmire.

Within the grassy meadows, Little French meanders substantially and presents a classic trout fishing opportunity. But that opportunity was limited to three- to six-inch brook trout, which disappointed me greatly. Beaver ponds have flooded much of the meadow and the meanders are not surmountable, because they're deep and crossed by rotted, burned, and barkless, slimy trees. Moreover, these meanders wind from the forest edge on the west side of the meadow to the forest edge on the east side, so they filled the meadow, forcing me back into the forest. At times, I thought I'd found a trailette running through the forest for a while, but found it to be a damned trap! My choice seemed to be climbing over fallen trees or climbing over slim, fallen trees with water below.

*Middle French Creek.*

From Fisher Saddle at 7,500 feet in elevation to Trail 504 at around 6,000 feet, this was my experience of hiking Little French Creek, and my shins told a sorry tale: they were scratched, poked, pumiced, scarred, abraded, and otherwise bloodied until I found a cross trail. Trail 504 was managed by the users of motorcycles and took me on down to 4,500 feet.

Trail 504 was a godsend! I have never been so delighted to find a walkable trail. When I slept beside the creek at the end of the meadow and called out with my best wolf howl, it was answered by a pack of wolves on the west side of Little French. We traded howls until I realized that I might be hunted, at which point I shut up and went to sleep as well as a Little Red Riding Hood could.

The next day I hiked on motorcycle trails that ran up and down this 90,000-acre roadless area and eventually came to Jenkins

*A rickety bridge over French Creek.*

Crossing. This is the place where logging trucks would have rolled in to cut the trees along French Creek 20 years ago. The road stops, thankfully, at the bluff high above the creek, and a trail bobsleds down to the creek. I hiked down from Jenkins Crossing to Jenkins Crossing bridge, about 1,500 feet below, to where the trail crosses the larger French Creek. The Jenkins Crossing bridge was one of the major reasons that I chose to hike in this drainage. This bridge was built by acquaintances of mine more than 20 years ago and has run its course. I mean that it is dilapidated and threatens to fall down every year. It exists only by the grace of God, the people who originally built it, and those who have repaired it over the years. I wanted to see what condition the bridge was in at this point.

The Forest Service had planned to replace it with an engineered metal bridge that would be flown in place and would last damn near forever. That sounded absurd to me, and I challenged the Forest Service's plan for this "flying bridge," as it is mainly useful for motorcycles. Others could wade the creek when it was not at flood stage. I hoped that my challenge would force the Forest Service and all of the bridge users to consider the alternatives to a metal bridge. All that needed to happen was for a group of people to focus on rebuilding the bridge by cutting the logs and boards to create the treads. This bridge in the wilderness could easily be rebuilt with the sinew, tenacity, and moxie of its users. In that manner, its many users could talk about its use, how it would be paid for, and who would maintain trails for hikers as well as motorcyclists. All that we needed was a well-designed wood bridge that could carry people, horses, and motorcycles. The bridge should be the work of the people who plan to use it. However, the Forest Service insisted that it must be engineered and that the best way to guarantee the safety of its users was to use the flying bridge.

After crossing the bridge at Jenkins Crossing, I hiked up French Creek on a fine but steep trail (#116) about four and a half miles to what had been designated Trail 308. The trail went for a quarter mile and then became a classic trailette, and in a blink it had vanished. Trail 308 had not been maintained for many years, and trees had fallen across it and brush had grown over it. I slept on the decision of whether to go up French Creek or to bail out to Jackson Creek and the road to McCall. If I bailed out, I would have to hitchhike back to my truck at Fisher Creek Saddle, and that would take me the bulk of the next day. If I continued hiking, I had two choices: the first was to bushwhack up the French Creek drainage; the second was to take a high-country route and hike cross-country to Black Tip Mountain at 8,290 feet and then simply drop down to my car from there. When I awoke, I felt like hiking, so up I went.

I will not bore you with the harrowing events that the trail presented other than to say that the French Creek route was nearly impassible. It was no longer a trail, and the route was steep. The high-country route was possible after tramping through six miles or so of annoying cross-fallen trees and up some hideous elevation gain. About the latter point, however, I have to admit that I never took the time to calculate how much elevation I would lose and then gain to reach Fisher Creek Saddle from French Creek. However, at a later time I realized that I had lost and regained about 4,000 feet—8,000 feet in total, most of it off-trail. I was tired and beat; I moved slowly up to Black Tip, and I hiked all day (with long breaks in the hot weather). I certainly felt it more than I would have in the halcyon days of my youth. I passed Trail 504 on its merry way over Center Ridge and continued trudging toward Black Tip. Finally, the forest gave way to alpine terrain and easy hiking.

Right. Easy hiking! Up and up I went, dancing through stacks and piles of fallen trees. I stopped to get water from several snow patches and saw an expansive view of the Salmon River Range stretched out from horizon to horizon: Bear Pete Mountain, Storm Peak, North and South Loon Mountains, Beaverdam Peak, Lick Creek Summit,

Fitsum and Nick Peaks, Buckhorn Mountain, and on down the line to the south. This is what some called the Salmon River Crest, but in anyone's view, it is fabulous.

Still, Black Tip, rising like an isosceles triangle, couldn't be climbed by me, so I had to go down and around Black Tip and rise again on its shrugging shoulder. The scree down and up would cost me another 1,500 feet, but it was pretty to be sure. Pretty damned tiring is what it was. In a pretty remote place. But with that climb behind me, I envisioned my truck before me. I had to make another decision: to go downhill or to follow this ridge around several mountains and go down to where I figured I'd parked my truck. Not that I could see it though; it was a bright figment of my imagination. But I knew it was only three heartbeats away.

Of course, I chose to hike the easier route—downhill. The way was paved with flowers: penstemon, lupine, sego lilies, and Indian paintbrush. At one point I rode on bending willows in the way that Robert Frost, the poet, saw a child doing with

*Black Tip Mountain in the 88,000-acre French Creek roadless area.*

birches. That was joyous, if painful, and soon I would be at my truck in this perfect world. But I found no road at the end of my rainbow, and with no end there would be no truck. With no truck there would be no beer. I felt confused and was unwilling to accept that I had made a mistake that left me in the wrong drainage. I had turned the wrong way, and the evening was quickly bringing darkness. Now seemed an opportune time to look at my map and compass and figure out where the hell I was. I located a cone of land where I might be and planned to head up toward Black Tip and retrace my steps. But first I looked around for the road. No dice. No road. Still the same mistake. No hope to get out before tomorrow. Another thousand feet up. Tomorrow.

My girlfriend would worry, and my boss at work would be angry. Shit. I was out of water and food and I had to come up with priorities. Water. Place to sleep before dark. Climbing up to call with my cellphone would wait. So would the beer. Unfortunately.

It was dark as I lay down in a meadow, beside a small creek, below the ridge that I would climb tomorrow. I slept the sleep of the fool, but in comfort. I woke at dawn, stuffed my gear back into my backpack, and got to walking. When I reached the ridge, it looked a lot longer and bumpier than I had anticipated. Glad I didn't try that one last night. That day I ridge-walked, left a message for my girlfriend when my phone worked by some modern-day miracle, as I hiked along the ridge. I moved forward until 9 a.m., then 11, then noon. Still no road and no car. In a couple of places, I stopped to wet my whistle on snow patches. I knew that this was the right way to my car. I knew it. I just knew it. It had better be. Several unnamed mountains lined up along the ridge, and at last a fairly level patch of land and the road came to into being as if out of the clouds. Then the truck. I stumbled to it.

I drank two beers with incredible relish, ate peanuts and M&Ms, sat thankfully in my truck, and thought about my four-day hike. French Creek was a tough stroll, because it was heavily burned and trees had fallen down across the "trail," making it a lost drainage for more than 20 years. But the French Creek roadless area is a treasure that should be bragged about—it should be a wild river, trails should be managed for motorized and nonmotorized users, and the land should remain wild rather than be roaded and logged. It should not remain a hidden paradise, if a paradise it is to you. I held the dregs of the last beer in a coffee cup, turned the key, and headed down the long, bumpy road toward civilization.

# HIKING ON THE SOLSTICE

The summer solstice is the day that provides the most light to walk by each year. Rising at dawn east of easterly and falling west of westerly, the sun shines directly overhead at noon and falls, seemingly rolled by gentle gravity, into brief hours of darkness from around 11 p.m. to 5 a.m. The summer solstice is not the best day to travel in the high country of Idaho because it also tends to be the day with the most snow melting—rivers and creeks are running high, weather is unsettled, and warmth is just catching up with the long cold darkness of winter. It is usually a fiery day that brings a smile to every face, but sunlight is slow to warm the earth, and like scalding water poured on an ice block, the snow goes quickly once the melt begins. The warmth speeds its effect exponentially as summer progresses. For that reason I planned to do my solstice hike a month later than the solstice, in July, having learned a lesson in the high snows of 2009, 2010, 2011, and 2012.

I guess I shouldn't call it a solstice hike then, because I'd learned from previous solstice trips that July might be the better time to hike in these mountains. Actually, I knew that this plan would be a good one as it responded to my former girlfriend's concerns about making poor decisions on my solstice hikes. It was the proper and reasonable response to many difficulties resulting from those fine, scary, fun, and mostly unexplainable hikes which usually ended up with a shrug of my shoulders when asked why I went. "Not really sure why, Sue" never seemed an adequate answer. However, I learned that there is never an adequate answer to the whys in life. I could've made plans to walk in snow-free lands or flatter places but, nah, why? After all, I wasn't planning to climb a Douglas fir tree in hurricane winds to test my mettle, like some latter-day John Muir.

I started out at Boulder Meadows Reservoir, hiked up to Boulder Lake, and on between Buckhorn Summit and Buckhorn Mountain, over the lowest pass, at 8,159 feet elevation. I saw no snow in this dry year and worked up and down across a steep, handsome, rugged scree slope over toward Buckhorn Mountain Lake several

*Pictured Left: Full moon over Buckhorn Mountain.*

miles distant. For a short hike it sure seemed long, and after hiking up 500 vertical feet I looked over a view point and recognized that I had to descend 500 feet and another 500 down to get into a valley between where I now stood and what should be Buckhorn Mountain Lake. I didn't see the lake, but I knew it was beyond yon ridge looking about twice removed from hideously far. I'm not saying that 1,000 or 1,500 vertical feet is all that much to climb, but I'll admit to a vague form of intense disappointment and will deny that age has one single thing to do about it. But my, oh, my, it seemed like a long, hard trek that stood before me. I sat down and groaned, ate from a bag of miserably wet raisins and peanuts, moaned about having to give up more elevation than I had gained and, worst of all, I would have to gain that same elevation a second time to be at the freakin' lake.

Buckhorn Mountain Lake.

Reluctantly, eventually, slowly, I took the plunge, limping slightly as a reminder to enjoy my self-pity. Oddly, the down portion became the hardest part of the trip, well, until I had to go back up, because it pounded my toes, but I was in bliss when I crossed a meadow full of wildflowers all, it seemed, in full glorious bloom. Water squished up with every step. I took a cool drink from the meandering creek and headed uphill again to get closer to this distant, ethereal, beckoning, and entirely theoretical mystical lake above me. Was it a pretty trip? Sure it was! Pretty painful.

I soldiered on. There was hardly a sign that people had ever visited Buckhorn Mountain Lake when I lumbered up to it, but the fishing was superb and the scenery inspired my mind. It's a small lake, maybe 10 acres but very deep, and every fish I caught was roughly 16 inches, rainbows that weighed at least a fat pound. They were most likely planted by an airplane three years ago as fingerlings. That was the human impact—airplanes in the backcountry—but a clear benefit for me.

I walked around the lake, took a dip in it, had a short sleep beside it, skipped stones in it, and had to leave it for home within the hour. I devised a better plan to return to this lovely, nearly invisible and

unvisited lake next year. I would forget the steepness of the last mile or two (just chock it up to a demented memory), camp beside the lake, and get to know its beauty. The seven-hour hike was worth it but it was only half over at 4:30 p.m., so I made a much better plan for the next year. But don't even think to ask.

*Pink monkeyflowers.*

The long summer solstice fleeted. That is always the way that nice things seem to work: one must leave a cherished place somewhat unknown to recognize that rarity increased its value enormously. Realistically, I might never get here again, so I wanted to know something, no, I wanted to know everything about this land that I'd walked upon, this place that I'd seen and the water that had offered me fish. The air smelled bitter and sweet with lodgepole pine pollen, a smell that fills your head with sneezes. I idled there a bit, cleaned the redolent fish, felt a warm wind that scribed the lake water below me, lingered and ate handfuls of M&Ms and a few fresh huckleberries. This basin expressed friendliness, but shadows of the peaks grew and the last breeze chilled my neck. Still, it was an effort to pick up my pack and walk away from Buckhorn Mountain Lake.

An osprey landed in a small whitebark pine snag beside Buckhorn Mountain Lake. She called and called and called in that wimpy, complaining voice of hers before lifting off. She seemed to be scolding me for finding and catching fish in this lake. As if it were her own damned home! I held up my three big rainbows to her and yelled to her "Don't you wish?" as she flew away to another basin far, far, far away. I stuffed the fish into my daypack and headed down the outlet creek from Buckhorn Mountain Lake to Buckhorn Creek and up the creek just as the sun set. The unnamed tall, rocky peaks rose in cirques on either side of Buckhorn Peak at the headwaters of three drainages. That confused me: there were three drainages, not two, along with the trail being under snow. I wasn't thinking that a trail ran through the pass beside Rapid Peak. The mountains held a mystic glow on their backs, side-by-side like brothers and sisters crystalized in this nameless range of spectacular mountains. This place is home for elk and wolves, salmon and bull trout, wolverines and bears. And one pissy, pointy-winged, complaining osprey. It should probably be called the Buckhorn Range, right?

I saw 20 kinds of wildflowers, from shooting star and columbine to larkspur and blue gentian, on this trek from fairly low to higher elevation areas and back, from forests to alpine heather and scree. I saw wildlife from hawks to black bears and forests from big old Ponderosa pines to lodgepole pines to the higher elevation whitebark pines. Some of the forest was burned and some was not. It showed a healthy mosaic pattern. There was plenty of water everywhere.

These solstice hikes have become for me a symbol of brilliant days of summertime in the mountains of Idaho, the power of being alone in wild places with wild life, and of the will of nature to heal what otherwise we are killing. Sometimes it was clear that nature was a killer too, if her warnings were not heeded, but the summer months were verdant and vital, young and full of joy, and these feelings soothed me.

Buckhorn Creek is the dominant drainage in this vast unprotected wilderness; it is the heart and soul of the land, the light and dark, the hot and cold of daytime, the source of water, and the flow of its seasonal consciousness. Buckhorn may be a word that some crackpot from Idaho first used to describe this place. You may argue about its name with fellow hikers but that will change nothing. It is a term that speaks of the respect that I have for this land and everything it supports because I know where Buckhorn Creek is. Call it what you will: it is a wilderness of rock, animals, and vegetables. These mountains don't much care.

*Huckleberries may save your life!*

I moved onward to Boulder Lake, a long, clear hike in twilight, and left this wild world to the osprey, fish, flowers, and huckleberries. On the trail from Boulder Lake to Boulder Meadows Reservoir I walked and stumbled in darkness between lodgepole and whitebark pines with a summer solstice moon to lead my way. As always, I wandered through darkness to find my home under these perfect mountains.

# IN THE LAND OF THE
# MIDNIGHT SUN

*David Brower, as executive president of the Sierra Club in 1956, was directed by the club's board of directors to accept the construction of Glen Canyon Dam in return for two planned dams in Dinosaur National Monument that would be scrapped. And that was done. In 1963, he wrote, "Glen Canyon died and I was partly responsible for its needless death. Neither you, nor I, nor anyone else, knew it well enough to insist at all costs it should endure. When we began to find out it was too late." Today, we know that the largest piece of public land in the United States with unprecedented numbers of wildlife, the National Petroleum Reserve in Alaska (NPR-A), should endure. But will it?*

Eight of us landed in the 23.8-million-acre National Petroleum Reserve in Alaska hoping to see the biggest, wildest, remotest place in the United States. It is managed by the U.S. Bureau of Land Management on behalf of the public and my fellow adventurers and I did not want to see oil derricks and pipelines; we'd seen plenty of those in Wyoming. What we saw as we flew in to land beside the Nigu River, a tributary to the Colville River, were castellated mountains and winding rivers in the Brooks Range. Floating down the Nigu, we watched grizzly bears prowling, herds of caribou strolling along treeless hills, moose moving slowly across the tundra, and peregrine falcons perched on cliffside nests feeding their young. Loons, arctic terns, sandpipers, and jaegers flew around our campsite, which became nearly flooded by high waters. Archeological sites showed centuries' worth of evidence of Indigenous Inupiat settlement. I had hoped to experience this vastness, a place as wild as wild can be, once in my life. And it did not disappoint.

There's a reason the NPR-A, also known as the Western Arctic Reserve, topped my list of places to see. In December 2019, a newly formed company called North Slope Exploration leased one million acres from the Bureau of Land Management to explore and develop the land in the Reserve for oil. This added to 1.4 million acres that are already wide-open for development. According to a November 2019 BLM

*Pictured Left: A moment of peace in the National Petroleum Reserve in Arctic Alaska in the Brooks Range.*

Environmental Impact Statement (EIS), the Trump administration was poised to further reduce protections for the Reserve, and offer more tracts for additional oil development. In 2020, they sought to do exactly that.

But please let me explain, before I go on, what the Reserve is. The Western Arctic Reserve lies west of the Trans-Alaska Pipeline, which is flanked on its east by the 19-million-acre Arctic National Wildlife Refuge. Alaska's Arctic ecosystem includes the Brooks Range, which runs east and west, with dozens of rivers running north to the Arctic Ocean. This area is roughly 67,188 square miles, larger in size than New York State, and is marked by a spectacular geography of mountains-upon-mountains and then leagues-upon-leagues of coastal flats. Behind us 7 million acres of the Gates of the Arctic National Park and Noatak National Preserve stretched to the south. We had flown 350 miles north from Fairbanks, the most northern big city in the States, a hundred miles beyond the Arctic Circle, and through the vast and rugged Brooks Range to the Nigu River. This river runs north into the Etivluk and the Etivluk into the enormous Colville River, each of them a winding watercourse born to taiga and tundra and married to fathomless solitude. When the plane departed for the last time, this land felt to me as if it was endless.

The BLM's most recent EIS on the fate of the Western Arctic Reserve effectively outlines two choices: maintain this wilderness habitat or develop a big part of it for oil—the latter would likely see its 23.8 million acres diced into smaller pieces divided by roads and development. "It was prudent," said Alaska's state BLM director Chad Padgett, "to develop a new plan that provides greater economic development of our resources while still providing protections for important resources and subsistence access."

What may have been most "prudent," in Padgett's parlance, was U.S. Geological Survey scientists' 2017 discovery of 8.7 billion barrels of oil within this Reserve. Yes, you've got that right, that's 8.7 billion barrels of oil, an unimaginable amount of oil under the ground in the Reserve. That puts it in the realm of Saudi Arabia's oil reserves. The proposed "exploration and development" stands to further exacerbate thumbprints of climate change in the vulnerable Arctic and threatens much of this landscape's abundant wildlife. It will determine the future of the largest piece of public land in our country.

△△△

Once we gathered at the launching point of the Nigu, our group had 10 days to get to know one another and the Western Arctic Reserve, the Petroleum Reserve. We were a congenial group of diverse people from far-flung parts of the country. On the second night, after our group landed on the Nigu, Pat Henderson, one of our two guides, finished his duties for the night: the dishes were clean and tomorrow's breakfast was prepped. It was 11:30 pm and Pat shot me a big smile and said, "Let's hike." I laughed but he convinced me that it would be a most excellent walk under the midnight sun, so he and I took off on an unmarked route to an unnamed lake a few miles away. The midnight sun gave this landscape an ethereal quality that lasted all night rather than the two golden hours that are celebrated in more southerly climates. I wanted to catch a few arctic char or grayling and we hiked through a matrix of tussocks, those cursed foot-tall pedestals of grass formed by the expansion of ice, spaced about a stumbling foot apart.

Up a hill we tromped to set a course toward the lake. Pat looked at his GPS to make sure we had a bead on the right lake out of many in front of us and led us through more tussocks and boggy land. The walking was tough and tore at my Achilles tendons with every awkward misstep I took. But we walked beside blueberry bushes, stopping now and then to take a handful of the rich berries, and that

Aqpiks, or cloudberries, have a wonderful taste.

made up for much discomfort. There were berries of many types: cranberries, bear berries, raspberries, and odd-looking succulent tidbits called cloudberries. All of them filled us with energy.

On the way we saw two pomarine jaegers, birds that worked in a team effort to swoop, terrorize, and scream at what we soon came to realize was a smaller bird's nest. From where we looked it appeared that one jaeger chased the bird from its nest while the other, following, looked for eggs or the bird's young to eat. It was a desperate moment for the attacked bird and a smooth routine for the two jaegers. But it was over before we got to the nest, and the jaegers

flew on. After we passed this bird drama, we came upon some kind of ruined structures on another ridge. Pat suggested that it might have been a fence meant as a trap for caribou. Apparently, the trap was set by arranging sticks and rocks in upright positions, guiding the animals into a manmade corral from which the caribou couldn't escape. Then the hunting group of people would kill the trapped caribou with spears, knives, and arrows. This setting, so lonely, and so certainly arranged by a group of anonymous, wayfaring hunters in times past, had traveled many miles to set this trap on the off-chance that the caribou would come this way. It seemed like magic had happened here many, many years ago, but the people had vanished. Just then four caribou wandered lackadaisically on a nearby ridge.

Rain began when we came to the large lake and then torrential rain poured in buckets. Wind blew hard, forcing us to lean into this invisible force, and then it blew with gale force. Each drop stung. I made many casts into the wind and lost two of my very best lures but never caught a single fish. Going back to our camp seemed very long indeed through the harsh wind and rain, but somewhere in that stumbling, tussocky, drenched ground, which we walked with our heads down, Pat stopped and stood still. "Mike...." I looked toward Pat and he pointed at 200 caribou that had appeared out of the landscape like a mirage. We watched in silence as they parted into two smaller herds and heard the rumbling of hooves on the turf like the sound of rolling thunder; it must have been like the thundering sound of bison on the plains of South Dakota 200 years ago.

"Did you see that?" I asked after they were gone. Of course he saw them! I was astounded by the tramping sounds of the herd and its presence out of nothing. And then they simply vanished.

"Yeah, caribou."

"Hundreds of caribou."

"Yeah." Pat paused and lifted his hands into the sky. "They split like that scene of Moses, right out of the Bible. Just like that!" We laughed and drove on in this biblical storm to our soaked campsites. I thought about how the Inupiat might have angled that herd into their trap. When I turned in it was 2:30 am and sunlight shined, still as bright as a summer day.

△△△

Further oil exploration would particularly heighten the already intense conflict around the 3.65-million-acre Teshekpuk Lake Special Area and its globally significant bird population. Federal BLM assistant secretary of land and minerals management Joe Balash stated that geologists view the area as "extremely prospective." "The big question is," Balash said, "can we make some of that acreage available in a manner that is responsible and honors the subsistence way of life that the people who live in the NPR-A have lived for thousands of years?" But then in December 2019, North Slope Exploration purchased 83 oil leases, each roughly 11,000 acres, southwest of Teshekpuk Lake.

"It's a chess game of incremental moves," said Susan Culliney, policy director for Audubon Alaska, who adds that the new EIS puts some of the most vulnerable places in the entire Reserve at heightened risk. "This is how places get developed—it's slow and steady, a spiderweb of development." Another concern for this ecosystem is the increase in global warming, perhaps most pronounced in Arctic regions. The precise environmental effects will depend on where oil is found and how sensitively it is extracted, pumped, and piped to the Trans-Alaska Pipeline—as well as on the condition of melting permafrost.

The National Petroleum Reserve in Alaska is, for good and evil, bound by its name. In 1923, only four years after WWI's end, President Warren Harding designated, by executive order, this vast block of public land as an emergency fuel supply for the military. Since then, however, the Reserve had seldom been used as a military supply source. In 1977, Secretary of the Interior Cecil Andrus established three protected "Special Areas" under the authority of the 1976 Naval Petroleum Reserves Production Act: Teshekpuk Lake, Utukok River Uplands, and the Colville River. This law also allowed for "significant subsistence, recreational, fish and wildlife, and historical or scenic values" to be set aside for "maximum protection." And it balanced those conservation measures with oil exploration elsewhere in the Reserve. In 2004, Interior Secretary Gayle Norton added 97,000 acres of Kasegaluk Lagoon on the western boundary of the Reserve as another Special Area to maintain populations of beluga whales, walrus, seals, and polar bears.

The Reserve presently includes hundreds of miles, from the Colville River to the Arctic Ocean, with undisturbed habitat for many thousands of waterfowl—like king eider ducks, tundra swans, and white-fronted geese—on hundreds of ponds and lakes. What some might call barren ground provides homes for grizzly and polar bears, wolverines, arctic foxes, and musk oxen. According to Rebecca McGuire, avian ecologist for the Wildlife Conservation Society, the Arctic coastal plain boasts higher species diversity and density of breeding birds than anywhere else in the circumpolar north. "The NPR-A is the most important part of the Arctic coastal plain for breeding birds," she said.

Another concern for this ecosystem is the increase in global warming that is most pronounced in Arctic regions of the world. This warming is closely tied to carbon emissions that have blossomed over the past 200 years, since the beginning of the Industrial Revolution, and today are showing alarming effects. An AP article that went out in August of 2019 noted that Alaska's air temperature was 5.4 degrees above the long-term average for July, its fire season was extended by at least a month, and that sea ice in the Arctic, which provides habitat for polar bears and walrus, had "retreated to the lowest level ever recorded for July." One month later a second AP article reported that the sea ice had disappeared entirely in offshore Alaska.

However, peregrine falcons, classified as endangered 50 years ago, currently enjoy the excellent habitat in the Arctic, with little pollution and good breeding terrain on the cliffs of the Colville River. This fueled their recovery to hundreds of mating pairs in Alaska. In 1999, the U.S. Fish and Wildlife Service removed these birds from the endangered species list. Along with hearty salmon runs, remarkable archeological sites, and major fossil beds, rare migratory waterfowl and shorebirds are found along the Colville River each summer. Musk oxen, too, reintroduced a few years back, once again thrive in the Reserve. How long they will persist no one can say.

△△△

Pat Henderson, the guide, said, remarkably casually, as the group was unpacking at our fourth campsite, "Hey, Mike, look." He pointed beyond the two rafts. "There's a grizzly bear across the river." I told Kevin and Kevin told his wife, Vicky. Larry Goldstein, the lead guide on this expedition, saw the bears as he was unpacking and stopped for a moment to look at them. He smiled at me. Kiliii Yuyan, a photographer for *National Geographic*, ran to set up his photographic equipment at the cobbled bank of the river. I looked across the 100-foot-wide, braided river and saw the blonde sow with

*A rock castle on Puvakrat Mountain beside the Etivluk River, a tributary to the Colville River.*

*A grizzly bear and her cubs beside the Nigu River.*

her two cubs. Four cameras came out and we all pointed them at the sight. "A grizzly bear!" I said. "Damn, she is beautiful."

The bear had a dark face in the midst of blonde hair and looked big beside her cubs. All of us stood looking at her for half an hour and finally decided that she might be too far away to be an immediate danger to us. It was more than strange to realize that the beauty of this grizzly bear, her cubs, and her seeming peaceful demeanor allowed us to ignore the danger that stood a mere 20 seconds away. Or less, at a gallop. But we were a tight group of eight and would be nearly impossible to attack. Nearly. The grizzly looked sidelong at us periodically as she ate grasses and willows, and we continued to watch her and her cubs, spellbound. Larry, the lead guide on this trip, looked carefully at her every action for a time as he served us a vegetarian dinner. I saw that he had a shotgun not far away if it was necessary. Fortunately, it wasn't.

△△△

Pure wilderness may be the Western Arctic Reserve's most defining characteristic, but it's also home to Indigenous Native Americans. Inupiat villages have existed within the Reserve for as long as anyone remembers. Forty years ago, an Inupiat spokesperson sent a document to the Secretary of Interior. "The Inupiat View" it said, served to demand "Free access and use of the homeland by Inupiat villagers; Strict protection of the homeland's physical, biological, and cultural environment; [and to provide] the highest possible degree of home rule and management control of the homeland by the Inupiat." In addition, the View states, "National energy needs should not be transposed into a general exploitive policy ... [and] Development for oil and gas development should be really compact and carefully staged to avoid environmental and social overload." In return, the Inupiat received a "statutory framework" from the U.S. government promising to meet those requests.

But that framework has sprung leaks under the pressure of additional oil profits and an oil development–happy administration. Today, the Inupiat have divergent opinions within the community—some oppose oil development while others support it—but even so, they are in agreement when it comes to the topic of maintaining their subsistence style of living. The town of Nuiqsut, for instance, is home to 425 inhabitants living in close proximity to the oil development that supports them economically; however, their wild surroundings afford them essential opportunities to hunt for caribou, whales, and to fish.

According to a 2017 report from the University of Alaska, McDowell Group, two million barrels of oil were produced at Prudhoe Bay in 1977. Twelve years later, 500 million barrels. "Today we are at one-quarter of that capacity (of 500 million barrels). That is the way of most industries." This pattern of depletion seems to be behind Alaska Senator Lisa Murkowski's urgency to drill. Addressing the Alaska Oil and Gas Association, the Republican stated, "We have to make sure that drilling will protect the environment and protect the wildlife and protect the land. That is our responsibility. But we will also have to be relentless." Within two years, Congress and the Trump administration had passed legislation requiring that oil exploration be done within the coastal flat of the Arctic National Wildlife Refuge, the renowned area across the pipeline from the Reserve.

ConocoPhillips, Alaska's largest oil developer, has holdings in lease units in the North Slope of Alaska including Kuparuk, Alpine, Mooses Tooth 1 & 2, Bear Tooth, Willow, West Willow, and Harpoon. The company also holds 733,000 acres of undeveloped land within the Reserve. ConocoPhillips acquired 48,000 of those acres in the NPR-A's 2018 lease sale, and another 33,149 in 2019. It now has virtual ownership of 1.2 million acres within the Reserve, according to company information. In 2019 the oil company claimed to be "a model for future developments," thanks to "directional drilling, zero harmful discharge, and other innovations to minimize the environmental footprint on the Arctic." In addition to a diminished footprint, ConocoPhillips stated that the newer development allows for greater efficiency, as fracking and directional drilling have resulted in 80 percent increases in Alaskan oil production from 2008 to 2015.

The BLM decision on the crucial land use plan, the Activity Integration Plan (AIP), made in July 2020, on the use of the NPR-A, defined the most land open to leasing (approximately 18.6 million acres, or 82 percent of the NPR-A). That decision stated, "The area closed to new infrastructure would decrease to approximately 4.3 million acres." That compares to the 2013 AIP that decreed 11.8 million acres of the Reserve open for oil development and defined 12 million acres off-limits to protect vulnerable wildlife. The plan had been a balanced plan for its existence, until 2020.

The new AIP eliminates the Colville River Special Area entirely, leaving this stunningly beautiful and productive river vulnerable to damage by building of roads, bridges, gravel mining, pipelines, and other development activities associated with proposed oil and gas development. Most of the Teshekpuk Lake Special Area's 3.65 million acres would be open to infrastructure aimed

*A piece of the unique wild country within the NPR-A.*

at developing oil and gas. However, it also defines the remaining special areas, the Utukok Uplands, Peard Bay, and Kasegaluk Lagoon, affording them interim protection from oil development actions. Moreover, the potential development is maintained for an oil pipeline across the NPR-A from the Chukchi Sea to the Beaufort Sea and connecting with the Trans-Alaska Pipeline. Twelve Wild and Scenic Rivers would be maintained in their current wild condition, and all other rivers in the NPR-A would be eliminated from further protection. Protection of the nearly 22 million acres of roadless areas is not discussed.

The upshot of the 2020 AIP is to advance oil development in the NPR-A, as all of this land is within Alaska's Petroleum Reserve. The value of wildlife, the sanctity of the Inupiat, and the dangers of climate insecurity, as a consequence of developing oil products, are discounted in the new AIP, in the new world. The 2020 plan would shatter the NPR-A's 23.8 million acres of unified land into smaller and more vulnerable pieces.

△△△

A couple days after Pat and I found the potential caribou trap on our midnight-sun hike, Larry Goldstein took us on a hike to another archeological site. Larry likes to give us just enough information to keep us thinking. He said that the first site was a circle of large rocks that had been set up high on a hill commanding a view of the surrounding country. It looked to me like a circle of rocks that I had seen in Wales. "Why?" he asked. Larry bid us silently to look around this hilltop and try to imagine what happened at this site. Then we gathered again and each ventured our thoughts about it. I suggested that it was a caribou trap like the one that Pat and I had seen, but this was more developed. Kevin, a professor, writer, and historian. asked if archeologists had been here. And what had they said?

*A lone caribou along the Etivluk River.*

After we all had taken our shots at understanding what this place had been, Larry said that he had read an archeologist's report of a similar place. A circle of stones, called a Qargi, was a spiritual place where Inupiat men had come to pray or perhaps to listen to a shaman sharing wisdom for their hunt. He said that this circle was last used roughly 500 years ago. The rocks that were set in a line below the Qargi might well have been a caribou trap. Larry pointed out the way the rocks lined up, and I imagined sticks standing up and held by the stones that would corral a herd of caribou into a pen. "What are the larger holes in the ground?" Larry asked. Maybe that was where hunters hid and jumped out with spears or arrows to kill the animals? Or maybe they were storage holes for food supplies. We couldn't say which they were.

I am no archeologist, and I don't know what the holes were. They were interesting to look at, but it was very hard to envision what the Inupiat people had experienced in this forbidding world and why they stayed so far to the north with six months of near darkness and bone stiffening coldness working at their souls. There must have been joyous times for people who lived off the land—making leather clothes, killing caribou for food, and on the coast, savoring the warmth of a whale's carcass, celebrating births, mourning tragedies, enduring the long arctic night for two months, and marveling at the brilliant green and red auroras oozing across the sky. Then came the longest day of summer and there might be a big feast of caribou. Or no food at all, depending on their divine luck. Some people might have starved. There must have been miserable days out in minus 40-degree cold with little snowpack on the ground. But the Inupiat were not here today to experience the summer beauty or to tell me their stories of what had transpired here. The land, however, told us much of the story that day as we looked out to the Colville River and the mountains beyond.

△△△

"Teshekpuk Lake should remain protected," Daren Beaudo, former spokesman for ConocoPhillips said, adding, "Other areas south of the lake that are currently unavailable for leasing could be made available for leasing without significant impact." Some of ConocoPhillips' conservation practices have included reducing the size of each gravel pad for drilling, from 65 acres in 1970 to 12 acres today, and using more drills in a single place to ensure access to a larger area. In 1970 each drill-pad drew from three square miles in an underground pool of oil, and in 2019 ConocoPhillips predicted that five drills, aimed diagonally from the pad, would grant drillers access to 154 square miles. We may soon see what oil interests can preserve in this odd, beautiful, and productive non-preserve—Teshekpuk Lake and its surrounding land—but I am convinced that ConocoPhillips wants to protect everything they can. Is it possible to have their cake and eat it too?

On February 2, 2021, newly elected President Biden proclaimed in Executive Order 14008 "that the Secretary of Interior shall pause new oil and natural gas leases on public lands or in offshore waters" to establish a review of the leasing that looks at climate changes and other impacts of development. This pause that the president has forced will stop the existing AIP for a moment and may allow the Biden administration to assess alternative values within the NPR-A, such as its world-class wildlife homes, its climate, and the place of the Inupiat. However, what will happen to the NPR-A remains in question with its formative proclamation defining petroleum as its main purpose. Clearly, oil development is only one purpose, but changing that proclamation would require a new law passed by an increasingly divisive Congress. It is an unlikely but possible outcome.

△△△

It rained hard again last night, and the wind blew at racehorse pace all morning. We decided to stay in camp until the rain let up. Larry called a meeting and we collaboratively made the decision to make a dash for the river at about 1 pm. As we floated, freshets flowed into the river in places where no channel was carved and lightning pummeled the ground in the Brooks Mountains behind us. Larry said that he had seldom heard of lightning in the Arctic. What would protect us in this leveled landscape of the coastal plain, with strikes of lightning all around us? Maybe tall willow bushes? Not likely. The wind and rainy squalls made each of us shiver as we floated down the Etivluk River.

Larry, reading the general feeling of people on the rafts, suggested that we stop to build a fire and eat some food to warm up. We stopped, made haste collecting wood, lit it with a flickering lighter, and stood beside the fire to warm us as we munched on candy. A full rainbow appeared on mountains to the east, then it was a double-bow, spanning the mountains that traded our misery for joy. The Brooks Range receded as we had floated and the majesty of clouds, mountains, and the land now sparkled with the new water. The foothills provided light in emerald and jaden hues.

We got back to the river and floated beside cliffs that were populated with hawks and falcons. One peregrine falcon flew and screamed at our rafts as we slowed to take pictures of it. Its nest had nothing in it and our boat quickly passed beyond it. Suddenly there was a newer nest and a young falcon stood in it, as defenseless as a downy, flightless bird could be. We stared at it and passed by quickly. No cameras had a chance to catch the moment. This land opened, not to boredom, but to greater wonders as the river-in-flood swept us 23 miles in no time to a place where we camped and warmed.

But chaos overcame us the next morning. Wind howled and flattened the cook tent. Vicky, Ray, Lynn, and I had been luxuriating in the calm of what the guides dubbed as "the Barn." The Barn stood beside the cook tent with our cups of coffee and small talk taking place when the wind hit like a hurricane. We all ran outside to see the cook tent turned inside-out. Pots and pans were tousled, the card-table overturned, and the big stirring spoons, forks, and knives lay helter-skelter on the ground. Larry stood beside the tent with a big cast-iron pan filled with hash browns and eggs, and with some sort of mercenary wisdom and a smile, he had caught the pan upright. The rest of us from the Barn gave a grand cheer for Larry's actions and rejoiced that the coffee pot still stood upright with its black-gold still intact. But the tent lay out in linear fashion and flapped like a

dragon in its death throes. So it goes in the wilderness. You can never judge the Arctic, Larry had said. It is always changing.

*Kiliii Yuyan under the luck of pure magic.*

We subdued the beast and hastily took down the Barn. Then most of the men took a hike towards Kingak Mountain in the rainstorm, with a hard wind, over more tussocks, and uphill beyond the river. The women were not so foolish! Half-way out Ray and I took a detour to a viewpoint that was much closer than Kingak and we sat on the leeward side of the mountain. We looked down on the Etivluk River and watched it twisting and turning across the land. Then we headed back to camp only to find that the river had risen significantly. Pat and Kevin were two hours behind us; they took a longer hike.

When Ray and I returned to camp, Larry had built an impressive dam to protect the cook tent in our absence, but, as all dams eventually do, this one leaked. Ray and Lynn moved their campsite to higher

*The Nigu River winding into the vastness of the Brooks Range.*

ground, such as there was higher ground on this small island! When Pat and Kevin returned to camp, they both hustled to protect their tents. Kevin and Vicky moved their camp to avoid inundation, leaving me with a first-rate view of disappearing riverfront acreage. Although Larry suggested that we sleep as evening progressed, I couldn't and walked regularly around this shrinking camp to check on rising water. When it rose, it created creeks across the island that was almost flat but had small gullies in it. Overnight no more creeks came through the island. Larry had monitored the water level all night and he said that the rise had slowed and was steady. I said, "Thank you, Jesus," for it seemed that we had nowhere to go but downstream if the river rose another six inches around us. Or three inches.

△△△

Wendell Berry wrote in his essay "Compromise, Hell!" that "we compromise by agreeing to permit the destruction only of parts of the Earth, or to permit the Earth to be destroyed a little at a time. ... Somehow we have lost or discarded any controlling sense of the interdependence of the Earth and the human capacity to use it well. ... There should be no compromise with the destruction of the land or of anything that we cannot replace."

The NPR-A will never be replaced once it is parceled out. Are we so economically dependent on the oil that will be taken from the Reserve as to agree to major compromises? Or can this land actually deliver its oil, as ConocoPhillips claims, still serving the people and maintaining wildlife: a minor compromise with great benefits? What will happen to Teshekpuk Lake, the lake whose name is virtually invisible to Americans? What would we support that will disappear, never, ever to return? Polar bears, beluga whales, peregrine falcons, or musk oxen? Certainly, we must beat our addiction to oil, and soon, or else we will end up dying from our addiction to it or killing for it. Any other conclusion is just a happy lie to ourselves.

Eight of us floated down to the wide Colville River from the Etivluk and camped there for two days, watched falcons and moose, rough-legged hawks, and another 10 or 15 caribou. I walked among willows following grizzly bear tracks, but not too far before turning chicken and walking back to camp. I compromised for the grizzly bear so that both of us might live. And clearly, we did; I wasn't eaten, and it wasn't killed for my sake. On the last day of camping in the NPR-A, the group waited for the plane to come as we pushed burning sticks into the ring of rocks and talked of things that might come. We all loved this place.

Eventually, a small plane came out of lifting fog and bounced on the gravel bar beside us. We greeted the pilot and he flew us again over the Brooks Range. Hundreds of miles of forest wilderness meted out below us as we skimmed the tops of ragged, bare mountains, and watched plumes from forest fires on the left and right. I feared for this long and lonely land in the Reserve; it has been a wilderness home for so many forms of life since time immemorial.

I remembered David Brower, the renowned conservationist, who, had he lived to see this moment, might have said, "Let's know that it is still not too late for this one American Arctic Reserve to endure! It can be protected without another compromise. Surely, it would be on behalf of animals and people who call the land home. In another moment, however, I was in a commercial jet, riding on that constant stream of oil, transported to somewhere in the midst of roiling human civilization, to my conservative Idaho home in Boise, thinking, "What will it take for us to protect things that we love and cannot replace?" Will we always save the toughest choices for last, until the flood rises to the point of a pending crisis? Will we always fear to say to oil companies: "Do not dominate another inch of land to produce more gasoline!"

**Each of the following five protected areas was created to maintain certain values as policy, but policy fails to protect them beyond what the most recent AIP dictates. Each of the areas should be defined and protected by statute. They are listed by size.\***

The **Utukok River Uplands** include more than 4 million acres, comprising the largest protected area in the NPR-A. It contains calving grounds and insect relief for the nearly 230,000-member Western Caribou herd (the largest in Alaska) and supports the highest concentration of grizzly bears in the Arctic. It includes large populations of wolves, wolverines, and moose. The Utukok River travels 225 miles to the Kasegaluk Lagoon and the Chukchi Sea. Many small villages above the Arctic Circle depend on the Western Arctic caribou herd for subsistence, while others depend almost entirely upon oil production jobs and production.

At 3.65 million acres, **Teshekpuk Lake and its surrounding wetlands** provide a seasonal home for many species of waterfowl: threatened spectacled and king eiders, yellow billed loons, dunlins, several varieties of geese, and others that are dependent on these wetlands. The wetlands also provide habitat for the 45,000 Teshekpuk caribou herd as they migrate. The eastern portion of Teshekpuk Lake has been hotly pursued by ConocoPhillips for oil exploration and production, and this protected area is currently feeling pressure for exploration. This is seen by many as the most threatened place in the Reserve, and two lawsuits have been filed to stop drilling. Environmental groups are challenging the six leases that were granted in 2017.

The **Colville River**, which has now lost its protection, consists of 2.44 million acres, with cliffs along the river supporting critical hunting and nesting habitat for gyrfalcons, peregrine falcons, golden eagles, and rough-legged hawks. The river flows 391 miles through the drainage to the Beaufort Sea near the Inupiat Eskimo town of Nuiqsut, and the area has a high wolf density. Here, grizzly bears, salmon, musk oxen, and caribou are hunted in a sustainable manner and, at the mouth to the Beaufort Sea, bowhead whales, seals, and polar bears are hunted as well. A major paleontological area and plentiful archeological sites exist along the river. Conoco-Phillips has developed two new oil fields that require access over the Colville River and has built a bridge over the river near Nuiqsut. That has opened this area for significant oil production in the future. What could happen in the delta of the Colville River in case of an oil spill is uncertain. Gravel sources, additional bridges, pipelines, and new roads also endanger the river in the near future.

**Peard Bay** consists of 107,000 acres at the point between Wainwright and Barrow, Alaska, and includes high densities of polar bears, ice seals, walruses, spectacled eiders, and red phalaropes, among other shorebirds. It also provides "haul-out" areas for ringed and bearded seals.

**Kasegaluk Lagoon** consists of 96,000 acres of wetland and water habitat supporting beluga whales, seals, walruses, and denning polar bears. This lagoon is said to be the largest undiminished coastal lagoon system in the world with its sheltered, shallow water and 125 miles of Chukchi Sea coast. The area supports the highest diversity of bird life in Arctic Alaska's coastal lagoons. Almost half of the world's Pacific black brant rest in the Kasegaluk lagoon annually. Beluga whales calve in its waters and up to 36,000 Pacific walruses "haul out" here. A pipeline route and a port development, already approved, could destroy much of the Kasegaluk habitat. The actual route has not been decided upon.

*Adapted from information supplied by the Alaska Wilderness League and National Audubon Society.

# TWO DEAD DEER

As I drove to Spokane out of Boise to perform the first reading from my new book, I drove alone. I was on the curvy road south of Riggins when I saw a ghostly gathering of deer, about five or six, standing in the middle of the road. They were shadows of stick deer dancing in the ice glare of dying sunlight and they were straight down the winding road. I slammed the brakes on and skidded and heard the screaming sound of tires. Swerved. Bump! Swerved back to keep the truck on the shiny road, glad that I just had my brakes adjusted and studs put in the tires. Bump!

I saw the first deer flailing in the ditch beside the road. I hit it head-on and it flew 20 or 30 feet to the roadside. It lay on the other side of the road. For a moment the other deer wasn't visible. I hoped that I had only given her a glancing hit and I pulled over to check the front of the truck, figuring the worst. Two people came out of their house on the roadside 200 feet away. They came with flashlights and calls of "Are you ok?" to see what had happened. They had heard the screaming car and the deeper bumping sounds.

The woman came first, walking quickly. "I'm fine," I said. "Do you have a gun? For the deer."

"No, no, I don't have a gun," she replied, surprised. She stopped and looked at me for a long while, calculating. "My husband does." She yelled back to him to bring a gun. "How's your truck?"

"I'm not sure." She gave me her flashlight, a big barreled one, aluminum and shiny, heavy with batteries. I went to the deer across the silent, steaming road. The flailing deer stopped writhing; it went still right in front of me as I watched. Her eyes looked suddenly lifeless—I can't explain what it was that death brought, but her eyes remained open, staring at the wild, wonderful, cruel world. That was her death, a sudden, eerie, violent death, the likes of which I'd never seen before. Her death was distinctive and I will remember the instant of her death. "I'm so sorry," I whispered, blindly, reverently to her. I looked around. How quickly this evening became inky. A pair of headlights flashed on their brights as I shined the flashlight beam at them. The car passed slowly.

The other deer was lying upright in the middle of the road, calm as could be. Her eyes looked down the road toward me. I had to get her out of the road immediately. Right fucking now! Cars swerved around her at the last moment. I waved my arms but when I came closer to her, she seemed to plead with her eyes and didn't move an inch. I had eviscerated her with my bumper and she lay in her guts on the road. The husband came toward me and stopped. Neither of us wanted to touch this slowly dying deer.

"Let's get her out of the road," he said. He grabbed one leg and I the other and we dragged her to the side of the road. Her eyes pled: "Do something for me."

"Can you shoot her?" I said. He pulled out the pistol and shot her once. She shivered, a bone rattling shiver. "Could you shoot her again? She's still alive."

"She will die quickly," he said. And she did. But her eyes remained open. "How's your car?" he said, obviously to change the subject.

"Lousy."

I checked my car: blood on the bumper, sticky with fur, front grill gone, radiator fine. "It's ok," I shouted back to him. He stood as if stoned. I called 911, reported the accident, and sought approval for the Fish and Game to "harvest" the deer for the man's freezer.

"My son will get it," he said. "I have Parkinson's and I can't do much."

"Ok. Well, I'm sorry."

"Me, too."

"I could help you."

"No, that's ok. My son can get the deer."

I got into my car which was still running, a significant miracle, and headed down to Riggins where I holed up in a little, cheap hotel and planned to have my car fixed the next day. I curled up feeling sick to my stomach and felt an inauspicious future. But for now there would be no more driving in the eerie twilight of Highway 95.

# WALKING UP THE BOISE RIVER

## *Part 1: From the Snake River Confluence to Caldwell*

Perhaps more than ever before, wildlife and people share space along the Boise River. Snowy egrets, great blue herons, red-tailed hawks, cinnamon teal and osprey, Canada geese and American coot, double-crested cormorants, turkey vultures, and pelicans are as common as house flies along the Lower Boise. In the cottonwood forests that line the river, deer, coyotes, and wild turkeys wander through the brush, and monarch, mourning cloak, and tiger swallowtail butterflies provide elegance.

Lands that are not easily accessible to people are often the very places where wildlife prosper. This is as true in the maze of inaccessible places along the Boise River and in the Boise bottomlands as it is in Idaho's Sawtooth Wilderness or in the nuclear research landscape at Idaho National Laboratory near Arco. It is also true that wildlife will congregate where there is adequate water and food available when both are scarce elsewhere. Water is more widely distributed in the Boise Basin since dams and canals have been operating, because every irrigation canal leaks and the water runs everywhere.

White settlers built farms on land that was good for only a few wild animals and turned it into productive habitat for people and crops. The Native American tribes that took the least from this land have lost the most in lives, resources, and happiness. As we've spread water in time and space to places where it didn't naturally occur, a few wild animals have gained from this. But sage grouse, pigmy rabbits, and anadromous fish are among the losers as the use of wild lands has changed. Cottonwood forests, some of the most productive forests in all of Idaho, have managed to prosper in the wet and dry lands of the Lower Boise River, but the yin and yang, the give and take, in this life-and-death scenario define what we have today.

△△△

*Pictured Left: The Lower Boise River in flood flow.*

In mid-May, as I walked along the Boise River near the Oregon-Idaho border, I spotted a man fishing for bass or catfish. We chatted and he posed for a photo. He may or may not have been aware that

nearby was the original site of Fort Boise, built in 1834 by the Hudson's Bay Company as a supply post on the Oregon Trail. The fort was abandoned two years later after severe flooding and too many skirmishes with Native Americans, and it was rebuilt in 1863, closer to a military post that is now the burgeoning city of Boise, and away from Indian raids. No one seems to know exactly where the original Fort Boise was sited, although there is currently a short, pentagon-shaped obelisk beside the river marking its approximate location. My guess is that what was left of the fort was swept away by one of the floods that occurred before the Boise River drainage was tamed by dams, before the flood control developments that today keep the water at bay.

The approximate site of Fort Boise, built in 1834. Soon after 1834, Fort Boise was swept away in a flood.

Agriculture dominates the current landscape along the Lower Boise. Canals, ditches, drains, laterals, and creeks are enhanced with water from the upper river drainage, and they thoroughly dissect the landscape and provide water to farmlands. They also make it nearly impossible to walk beside the river. Obscure ditches, as well as all of the named canals, often forced me to trace and retrace the river's path as I tried to head upstream. Many *"No Trespassing!"* signs gave the impression that no one should be walking beside this river at all.

A few weeks earlier, I had invited a few friends to join me on this trek along the Lower Boise. Some laughed it off, some wanted to hike a more scenic stretch, and some had other obligations, but none wanted to see the nether end of this river that was virtually in their backyards. Eric, my good friend, put it most politely in his e-mail note in response to my invitation: "Kind of you to offer! Plans prevent me from accompanying you on such an insane outing. LOL." Even my good friend Eric had deferred!

As I bushwhacked through 10-foot-high reeds and tough, but mercifully short, willows, I pulled countless numbers of cheatgrass seeds from my shoes and socks, I was bullwhipped by stinging nettles, and swore at arriving, once again, to a ditch full of muddy water and mayhem. Mosquitoes swarmed, ticks sneaked up my legs, and rattlesnakes and mudpuppies hid somewhere, I was sure, beneath my feet. It was slow going and, yes, I needed to come up with another plan! But not on this day, which was a cool and pleasant one, with the following day promising blistering heat.

Idaho state law provides that the land below the river's high-water level is owned by the public and is thus available for anyone to walk upon. But that doesn't account for the density of vegetation and many canals along the Lower Boise that would stop an eager beaver from passing where no trail has been built and maintained. Where was the high-water level anyhow? And what was I doing on this silly quest to walk the whole Boise River, from bottom to top?

I had decided that I was tired of traveling far away for each vacation when there was so much beauty right outside my door, and I wouldn't waste gasoline or time or money for this trip. A conservationist for many years, I had been working with local and statewide environmental organizations and *working on* federal and state agencies and a few stakeholders like ranchers, farmers, landowners, and developers, with the aim of improving the water quality of Idaho's rivers and lakes. I am a hiker, a fisherman, an occasional hunter, a has-been boater, and a writer, and I was just plain curious about the Boise River—my Outback. I knew there would be a great deal to learn about the river—not by what I was told, but what I could see firsthand on this hike, and I could learn most of it without having to travel very far. So, for that, I went walking.

Along the way, I stopped and talk to landowners, and they allowed me to proceed, without exception, across their properties, their roads, and the occasional levees along the river. I respected their wishes, and they were mostly kind, wishing me luck.

One man, who turned out to be a trainer of hunting dogs, ran out to me after I had knocked on his door, waited for a time, and then started moving on, resolved simply to continue my trespass upriver. No landowner much cared for me to trespass across his land, so I moved quickly, never looked back, and I never asked twice.

"Hey!" he called. "Where you think you're headed?"

"Upriver." I turned back and walked the hundred yards over to him. I told him I could just go around his property if he wanted. "The water is high and I'm sorry to trespass."

"Well, you're on my land."

"I realize...."

"How'd you get here?"

"I walked up the river, climbed a fence, came to your property, and knocked on your door. I didn't mean to just walk across your land."

"But you did." He scowled. "That takes some nerve."

"I had no choice." I looked at my muddy feet.

"Did you run into anybody else on your way here?"

"Yes, there was a man, Corey, who was rebuilding a pond for his cows and he told me I could walk over his land. We had a nice conversation and I gave him my card."

"He let you trespass? He's always been kind of strict about that. I can't believe it."

"He said I could walk over his land to get to the river. He pointed to the levee that I should follow. He said, 'Good luck with the next guy.'"

"Yeah. Well, I guess I shouldn't be the only bad guy that you run into." He chuckled a little.

"I don't mind. I can just go around. I'm really sorry."

He laughed. "Didn't look like you were going around. OK? Nah, you can trespass." He shook his head. "I won't make you go the long way around."

He looked sideways at me like a guy who was taking aim with a small-bore rifle. "You know you're the only person who's crazy enough to try to walk up the river. You're just nuts. People don't even raft down that river." He stood with his arms folded across his chest.

I laughed, as he continued: "Well, so, take the route beside the river, and be sure to close the gate. You have to lift it up on one end and latch it afterwards. It'll take some kinda move." He pointed to a white house in the distance. "You'll end up by that house over there with a bunch of dogs, and the guy may not be as nice as I am."

"Thanks. I am forewarned. I'll take the road after that." Then, in response to his further comments, I answered, "No. I don't like drones and I am not a U.S. Forest Service agent."

At the gate, I did some kinda move to close it properly. Pulled on it hard to make sure it latched. The man at the white house with dogs wasn't home. One dog was friendly, another barked incessantly, and a third just followed me suspiciously for a bit and eventually started sniffing at something else. I slipped by and took a road beyond the house. A small herd of cows in a pasture walked along with me; curious, and hungry, they were.

Later, I met a man who had just that day begun to irrigate a piece of land for the season. He directed the water with his shovel to every seeded furrow. He seemed the epitome of efficient water use as he widened and narrowed the water's path to help it reach thirsty corn seedlings. In other places, I saw the big machinery that had been used to work the land and make it more productive—mostly plows, planters, and harvesters.

Nearby, I walked through the little towns of Parma and Notus, indisputably agricultural towns. In Parma, the Crop Production Service seemed to have sprouted within a tall silo, beside tanks of undisclosed chemicals. A post-and-pole manufacturing plant, which made poles for fences, was nearby, along with hauling and harvesting machinery that were stilled and waiting for crops to grow.

In Notus, which is little more than a speck beside railroad tracks, I saw piles of new wooden pallets and shipping crates stacked three stories tall. An empty metal silo stood ready to store crops. The "Giant Produce" sign read, with hope, "Onions and Potatoes—Russets, Golds, Reds—Now Available." Neither a potato nor an onion was available

*Lower Boise River water being used for irrigation.*

at the moment, but the beauty shop was open, good coffee was flowing in the Garage Cafe, and the Senior Center offered brunch. Quesadillas were sold in a downtown joint. The Ten Commandments were listed on a sign attached to a fence. Cows were outstanding in their fields, and pivot sprinklers dampened the rich, valuable land. The water had already been brought in and the work in the fields was getting done. It was spring in the Lower Boise River drainage, and it was all Go! Go! Go!

I noticed that none of the water diversions from the river appeared to have screens to protect fish from entering the canals. I saw two large carp that had been stranded in a narrow irrigation watercourse, their corpses picked to the bone by vultures, coyotes, and flies, no doubt after the harsh sunlight had cooked their skin to leathery toughness. It seemed that the carp were able to swim to the smallest tributary of the irrigation system before it had dried up; that didn't bode well for any other fish in the Boise River.

Eventually, I noticed several live fish that had been trapped—big ones, flopping in an irrigation canal. A rookery of snowy egrets was alive, making eerie-sounding wails in the tops of a dozen cottonwood trees beside that canal. A red-tailed hawk screamed at me as I walked beside its nest. I realized that the hawks, ospreys, and coyotes would be beneficiaries of the fish that were caught and died in the irrigation system.

I continued out of town along the railroad tracks because I couldn't find a place to stroll by the river, after the canals and brush had worn me out. I walked beside sewage ponds marked with warning signs and through a marsh cut through by the railroad, finally trespassing on private land, through a massive gravel pit closer to the river, where mountains of gravel would be trucked out of the river basin. As fortune had it, no one was around to catch me trespassing here. Beside the gravel pit, mulberries grew on a tree next to a field of freshly cut hay that smelled wonderful. I ate mulberries by the handfuls!

After a while, I arrived at the levee. It was a great levee, the first really good levee I'd encountered on this river, and I was glad to be walking here because I was exhausted and it provided easy hiking. I read another sign that warned me not to trespass. I stopped and thought about how much public money had been spent creating upstream dams, the network of canals and levees that were built by the U.S. government, the price that Native Americans had paid when white people settled here, and the price paid by farmers and ranchers in the Lower Boise Basin. And then I ignored that fucking sign and walked on. It was outrageous to tell people to get off land that they had paid for to make productive. I understood that, and I hoped that a cop would too. I walked along the levee a bit, and then crossed the railroad tracks. I had arrived, at the end of this harrowing day, near the Rotary Park in Caldwell.

Before too long, I heard a freight train heading my direction. I sat down beside the track to take a photo as it approached. I caught it in the viewfinder as it seemed close enough to run me over. The massive train passed at 60-plus miles per hour, horn blasting, bright headlights rambling, and dust streaming away! *Click.* Perfect shot! Then I fell away, swept back by the force of the train and my sudden fear of this galloping machine that implied so much in the West. I was 6 feet away from a screaming behemoth that could have mashed me like the most miniscule bug.

*A freight train blew me away and galloped past.*

Now all I had to do was to get on my bike and ride through the darkness back to the point where I began the day. As I rode, I thought about how the Boise Basin was certainly a nice place to be a farmer. It seemed OK for the river to be like it was, even with all of the policy flaws that no one was motivated to fix. Who was I, anyway, to be concerned, when so few people even cared to look at this river as a living thing? I'm the fool! While my friends are out playing in the cool mountains, others are working the land, trying to make money for their families.

I realized that my life is the life of a gypsy, dodging from place to place to get by—and this time, thankfully, I had avoided capture.

*A girl swinging beside the Boise River.*

# THE PEACEABLE CANYON?

## *Part 2: From Caldwell to Highway 55*

The morning I resumed my Boise River walk, a few weeks after hiking the first section, I walked with Liz Paul, Boise River campaign coordinator for Idaho Rivers United, across the newly built Highway 16 bridge that spans the Boise River between Eagle and Star—the first new bridge across the river in more than two decades. The nearly quarter-mile-long, four-lane structure was deserted that day, being not yet completed. In this quiet spot, no lines were painted on the pavement, no signs told of the distances to upcoming off-ramps, and no traffic passed by.

The Idaho Transportation Department built the concrete bridge as part of a longer highway extension intended to accommodate increasing traffic movement north and south, as more and more people flock to the area to build houses. "Build it and they will come" seems to be the attitude.

"People didn't live beside the river because it was a series of gravel channels that were constantly changing," Liz told me. "The

bridge is a symbol of how hard it's been to get across the river," she said. In times past, the journey from the train station, across the Boise River, and into downtown Boise was a significant undertaking. The new bridge, however, "isolates people from the river," Liz said. Tall concrete posts raise the bridge from the wide and braided watercourse, and it is almost impossible to gain access to the river from the span. The bridge is an unfriendly thing, dedicated only to moving people quickly from place to place. But it could have been a beautiful thing that invited people to the river.

After Liz dropped me off in Caldwell, I began the second portion of my Boise River walk. Caldwell is a very civilized sort of place, with roads and railroad tracks, a lovely park, a clean shopping center, and a bike path beside the river.

At first, it was beautiful. But after walking less than a mile, I passed a flood-prone RV campground built too close to the river, houses built so close to the canal that I had to sneak around them and climb over a barbed wire fence to more forward, a dirty telephone booth junked behind some tumble-down buildings, and a graffiti-laden, smelly little reservoir that served as the point of departure for the canal. It was far from a perfect place to be hiking for fun.

I came to a sharp bend in the river that was forced by a basalt wall—the start of Caldwell Canyon. I'd never heard of this place until a few days ago, and I wasn't at all certain that it qualified as a "canyon." (Nobody would ever compare it to Hells Canyon on the Snake River, for example.) The river seemed pretty tame as I watched a family of geese floating gently along. But I could imagine what might have occurred 60 years ago after a big spring runoff. It must have raged when the flow was ten times what it was on this day of roughly 1,300 cubic feet per second, before the construction of upriver dams and irrigation canals. It would have been a surging, seething, rip-snorting, mad river eating at the basalt wall, flowing up and over the river plain, up and over what was now the RV park and irrigation paraphernalia.

As I walked along a minor road at some distance from the river, I noticed a sign for Curtis Park, which, as it turned out, was a very sweet, scenic place with a fine picnic spot and a long boardwalk leading to a marsh along a canal. Two-foot-long carp swam at a walking pace in the canal, breathing slowly, their sucker mouths opening and closing in moon shapes.

This place was slow, peaceful, and soothing. An osprey perched on its nest overlooking the marsh kept watch. This was a changed place, a winding walk, where monarch butterflies glided above the path and flickers flashed through broken sunlight. The sounds of traffic were muted by the trees, and no floods threatened.

But when I crossed a fence from Curtis Park and entered the adjacent, barren, cow-burned land nearer the river, it was again a changed place. The fence marked the divide between public parkland, verdant forest, and marsh, and a bare dirt, weedy, and thorny, sticker-strewn wasteland of private land. Beyond this parched dirt patch—it was only a quarter mile across—a rustic, private road passed through a lovely cottonwood and box elder woodland. As I entered this pleasant woodland, a pair of red-tailed hawks screamed to announce my presence.

The landscape's character once again changed quickly, however, as I crossed into fenced fields. Clearly, this landowner's economic survival was at risk. Why would the land be so variously managed in such a short distance? Perhaps one landowner was rich, and the other poor. One squeezed out every penny's worth of capital from the soil, while the other could afford to love the wildlife and trees. That is the way that I read the land, its poverty and richness reflecting those of its landowners.

I imagined a park following the whole length of the river, from the Snake River to the Boise River headwaters, and it was a thing of beauty. Let the whole landscape mirror the peace of Curtis Park, and it would once again be a fine place beside the river.

## Please stop shooting!

I was shaken from my meandering thoughts by the *bang-bang!*, *bang-bang-bang!*, *bang-bang!* pounding sounds of hammers and the bounce of nail guns, as unseen contractors built an unseen house somewhere up ahead. I walked about a mile along a dirt road beside the river as the sound of the nail guns got louder and louder, eventually becoming the blasts of shotguns. This wasn't the sound of hammers after all, as I had imagined. "Pull!" a man shouted. Then *bang, bang, bang, bang!* I imagined clay pigeons flying and bursting, and shotgun shells being ejected from the gun chamber.

"Pull!" a woman called. *Bang, BANG!* As I walked, the sounds grew closer, like cherry bombs being tossed at my feet. Suddenly war was declared, with shooting and shouting. "Pull!" *BANG! BANG!* There must've been a dozen people shooting, judging by the number of voices I heard. *BANG! BANG!* I couldn't see the shooters, but I imagined that they were now about 150 feet from me beyond the brush. How could that be?!

*Wait a minute*, I thought. *Maybe the shots were coming my way.* I retreated from the dirt road to a cornfield and stood behind some big trees and waited. *BANG! BANG! BANG!* After each shot, a fraction of a second passed before I heard the sound of sand thrown in the vegetation around me. The shots were incoming. They were shooting toward me! And with some accuracy, I should say.

"Hey, please stop shooting!" I shouted, fearing the scatter-shot.

"Pull!" *BANG, BANG!* The splashes of sand skittered around me.

"Quit shooting!" I screamed.

"Pull!" *BANG, BANG, BANG!* Maybe they couldn't hear me! Incredible. I heard them, why didn't they hear me? How close to me were the thousands of shot pellets? I saw nearby leaves shake and bits of dirt spring from the ground. Something stung my hand. No blood, thank heaven. This was an unbelievable moment. I waited behind a tree for the shooting to stop. It did. Maybe clay pigeons were being reloaded, or the shooters had run out of shot, or maybe they had heard me—whatever made them stop, there was silence and I took advantage of it to run like hell, jump over a barbed-wire fence and a ditch full of irrigation water, along the field, and quickly out of range of shotgun blast.

I hoped that the shooters never had a clue that I was within range. But I knew that I shouldn't have been there if private ownership means anything. And it did, and does. It could have meant my life,

Honk or be shot.

and almost did. I just wanted to walk up the Boise River, but this experience had made the path a bit more difficult, even if it was, technically, a legal route. Or so I would argue.

Walking through the field, where I was further trespassing, I came to an access road for the shooting range. A sign was posted: "Honk before entering Isom Island." A man drove toward the range, and I stopped him to ask directions to get out of there. "Could you tell me about where I am?" I asked, showing him my woefully inadequate map.

"No, I can't tell you where you are." He spoke gruffly and with obvious annoyance. "I just came out here for one purpose." I didn't ask him what that purpose was but thanked him just the same.

When another driver approached, I signaled him to roll down his car window. He anticipated my question, pointed vaguely toward the east, and said, "That way is the river." So I headed that way and stopped for a minute to eat lunch, ignoring a threatening sign that warned that trespassers tended not to come out alive, so don't come in. This was brutal, redneck country, and I knew I needed to get away as soon as possible. I walked on and was forced to trespass again to get closer to the river.

After walking a few hours, I reached a subdivision, where a woman confronted me. "You working with an agency?" she asked pointedly, dropping her shovel. She whispered something to her young daughter and walked toward me.

"No." I kept walking

"You're not?" she challenged.

I continued walking. "I just came from downriver and am heading to Atlanta."

"What's your name?"

"Mike."

"Why are you crossing our property?"

"I'm very sorry. I had no other way."

She didn't reply but was clearly unsatisfied. I kept walking with my back to her.

Half an hour later on the road, I ran into her husband, who had apparently talked with his wife about the stranger who had trespassed. He stopped me and asked, "Hey, do you mind talking with me for a minute?"

"No," I said. *Uh oh*, I thought. He explained that the Corps of Engineers had sent engineers of some stripe to look at their property without asking permission. They gave warnings and were apparently attempting to buy the couple's land. He wanted to know what, exactly, was my role in walking up the river and across their property?

"I'm sorry about your property," I said, and told him that I was a writer walking up the Boise River, and I hoped to relate stories of the people I ran into and the places that I saw. I don't think he believed me, but we shook hands, exchanged names, and parted ways.

At the next residence, a group of people were sitting on their porch, barbequing and bullshitting. I approached them very gingerly. "Excuse me," I said. "I'm walking up the river and I'd like to cross your land or else go around it." I was encouraged to go around, so I did.

The next house seemed quiet, and I knocked on the door. A woman answered, and I sheepishly told her my rap. While she was thinking about it, I said, "Have you seen the osprey nest across the field over there?" It was about 400 feet away. "There are birds on it!"

She suddenly softened. "Oh yes! They've come here for four years in a row! They are lovely birds, aren't they?"

"Yes," I said, glad to find a kindred spirit. We talked a bit and she let me trespass across her property. Then she mentioned something to her husband and he smiled. I waved and smiled and made tracks upriver.

Another mile in, I was tired, hot, and cranky. I'd been shot at. I was delirious after walking all day.

The River Ranch subdivision appeared to be laid out partially within the Boise River's flood plain. A canal ran through, and I looked for a bridge to cross over. The place was nice enough, with blacktopped streets waiting for cars, sidewalks and bike paths waiting for pedestrians, and fire hydrants waiting to extinguish flames. All of the landscaping looked as nice and as phony as it could be, with lawns sprinkled in green. No houses had been built here, however. It was like a ghost town, a creepy and petrified place. I passed through the empty subdivision, across the canal, and back toward the river.

## The mirage

After awhile, I walked into a wedding celebration, and then I arrived at the nicest levee I'd ever seen. It had been re-enforced on one side and defined the water level, where it looked safe and legal to walk. So I walked on the levee, which had been graded like a high school track. Beside it was a gorgeous pond—with sizeable fish swimming in it. Grass, brilliant green, stretched from the pond to a charming log cabin. All of this landscape was dreamlike, with storybook flowers and perfect irrigation; it stood out along the river as a place that invites a stroll through. *Someone loves this place*, I thought. I wished I could sleep in the cabin across the lake and gaze at the stars. But this was private land, and I had to move on quickly. A rich man's private property is no place for me to linger.

At the end of the day, as I traveled back home, I thought about the land and water outside my domain, defended by money, bullets, and tradition. The demands and uses of water and land seem set in concrete, so to speak, and would be hard to change. But I knew that changes were coming, as more and more of the Boise area became urbanized. The Boise River is defined by dams, diversions, and the ambitions of people who want its water. The river has given this arid place the possibility of life. As the river changes its course, it will change us too—swiftly and at flood levels.

## Another fresh start

The next morning, I started out fresh, near the Star Bridge, which crosses the Boise River a little south of the tiny town of Star. After I parked my car at the Star Riverwalk Park, and before starting the day's hike, I talked with a man who was fishing just below an unscreened diversion upstream. He said he'd caught an 18-inch brown trout and a smaller bull trout right beside the bridge. A bull trout? Seriously? I had my doubts, but he described the fish well and insisted that he had released it.

Bull trout require cold water, complex and clean habitat, and spawning and migration areas, and they thrive where salmon flourish, but salmon were prevented from entering the Boise River by dams on the Snake River. Bull trout were not introduced to the river by the Idaho Department of Fish and Game, and I doubted that they had survived in the Lower Boise River when it was low and warm in late summer in years past, but it was possible—and who was I to doubt what a fisherman tells me?

I also ran across Russ Renk, a man who was pumping up a raft beside the river. Russ told me he was an environmental consultant who had his own business in Washington State, but he and Dan, his brother, had grown up beside the Boise River near Star. Russ said that he had a record of fish catches going back 50 years, complete with the names of fishing holes, species of fish, and changes that

Russ Renk blows up his raft in preparation for another fishing trip on the Boise River.

had taken place on the river. According to Russ, from 1960 to 1964, he consistently caught rainbow and brown trout, bass, whitefish, squawfish, chub, catfish, bluegills, perch, and carp on spinners and salmon eggs, mostly on the Lower Boise River, the 60-mile stretch from Lucky Peak Dam to the Boise's confluence with the Snake near Parma. In 1960, he said, he took 97 fishing trips on the river.

Russ said that the Lower Boise had changed significantly over many years, mostly from increased flows in the river, which he believed had changed the slow-moving water habitat from one that supported bass to the a swift, clear-running water habitat that favors trout. Squawfish, chubs, and carp were prevalent 50 years ago, but not much else survived when the river's flow was severely restricted as dams were being repaired or maintained. What saved the fish during those times was the seepage and groundwater that managed to continue.

As the years went on, the Idaho Department of Fish and Game filed and won a lawsuit that ensured that water would remain in the river on a year-round basis for all wildlife. In 1960–64, however, there were plenty of trout, even a few bull trout, according to Russ.

Constructing the Diversion Dam, about 7 miles southeast of Boise, and Lucky Peak Dam, about 10 miles upstream, and a variety of other diversions caused major impacts on the Lower Boise River, causing the river to dry up (with the exception of gravel-pit ponds that were spared total desiccation) while dams were shut down for maintenance. The Diversion Dam diverts roughly half of the river in the summer for irrigation and delivers it through the 41-mile-long New York Canal to a wide network of smaller canals and finally to Lake Lowell, south of Nampa.

Lake Lowell is an odd place for a huge body of water, being on arid land, but it serves as a flood control basin and as a reservoir for agricultural irrigation, and it provides a good deal of boating, swimming, fishing, and bird-watching recreation. It is surrounded by the Deer Flat National Wildlife Refuge, which was designated by President Teddy Roosevelt in 1909. Homes have been built on the shores of the reservoir. All of the many virtues and conflicts inherent with construction of the reservoir and Deer Flat were created by water from the Boise River, and although each demand on the water there is carefully balanced, it must change when agriculture, recreation, or wildlife needs change. Fish and wildlife have been protected since 1909, but as of 2021, recreational users are rising in importance and residences are far more numerous.

△△△

As I continued my river walk near the Star Bridge, I took a picture of the river downstream, which looked very healthy, with much vegetation and many different channels of clean, cool water flowing swiftly by. I felt more positive about the river here in the middle of a community that seemed to support it. I walked along the Star River Walk, a mile-and-a-quarter stroll through the woods and fields beside the river. It was beautiful most of the way, although part of it needed to be rehabilitated to look natural; that plan is currently in the works.

*The Boise River looking good beside the town of Star.*

I walked over to a stout and well-crafted steel information sign to get myself oriented. One quote on the sign by Japanese conservationist Shōzō Tanaka struck me as profound: "The care of rivers is not a question of rivers but of the human heart." That spoke to me of compassion. The sign also imparted information about the goals of the people of Star; it read,

> The people of Star are committed to conserving the Boise River Corridor for nature-based recreation, wildlife conservation and flood control while protecting the quality of water on which we depend. The Star River Walk is the first step toward realizing our vision for the riparian heart of our community.

> Our goal is to develop a rich network of parks, trails, and open spaces that provide interpretative and educational opportunities as well as outstanding outdoor recreation. We look forward to the day the Star River Walk will stretch from Linder Road to Lansing Lane, linking existing Eagle Island trails to planned pathways in Middleton.

△△△

Some time later, in Boise, I asked Tim Breuer, former director of the Land Trust of the Treasure Valley, what Tanaka's quote meant, since LTTV was carved into the metal sign as a supporter. "That quote means a lot of different things to different people and that may be why it is good," he said. I laughed at the truth of that answer. Tim said that a portion of the land was purchased by the city of Star and that other parts are under an easement. "The river is the heart of the community," he said. "It's their front porch. They had no public land but they wanted nature, and access to the river, family floating, and fishing opportunities. Now it's a safe place and it's more naturalized."

A plow blade lingered in a field beside the Lower Boise River.

I mentioned that I had tried somewhat unsuccessfully to navigate the river by foot. "It's a different ask to bring the public across a piece of private land than to get one person across it," Tim said. I had to agree with him about that. "Connectivity along the river from the Snake isn't really possible right now for physical, ecological, and private property issues. It's nice to have big dreams, but we focus on what we can achieve right now," he added. *Yes*, I thought, *that was pragmatic and wise*.

△△△

As I continued my upriver hike, I could see that recreation use became more and more popular, more essential as the population had expanded, but some places had no access to the river. In some locations, the river backed up to houses; in others, a particular property right, such as gravel mining, blocked public access unequivocally. Signs were everywhere telling us where not to go. I believe that access to specific places on the river remains the key to its use for recreation, because, obviously, when a road leads down to the river, there is significant public use. Where there is no guaranteed access, there is no public use. Of course, we all want our special place to be unknown to others so that we might cherish it as our very own! So we put a fence around it. Put up signs. Keep the deadbeats out and allow only the angels to visit. But we all want to share your private place, and all of us are angels!

Along I went. An approaching fawn innocently bounded from the brush until it got about 5 feet from me, recognized that I was not its mother, stopped abruptly, and then bounded immediately away. Wild turkeys were everywhere in this half-used land.

Finally, I followed the oddly paved Meridian Road along the edge of a riparian cottonwood forest—a jungle along the river. Open grasslands graced the other side. I soon came upon low-income houses and trailers that crowded the river, and I had to crawl under the deck of one house simply to get by. (That house, by the way, is now gone.)

Eventually, thickets and a sewage plant made it nearly impossible to walk on the north side of the river, so I detoured to nearby Highway 44 for a couple of miles and tried to penetrate the vegetation at regular points. On one of those forays, I made

*A worker stands out in a newly irrigated field.*

it down to the river, but the areas both upstream and downstream were trackless and impenetrable, so I went back up to the road. I eventually found a bike path that led back along the river.

I saw many delights along that fine path: a rope swing; people swimming, playing, kayaking, drinking, and rafting; and not the least was a store that served me a chocolate milkshake that was oh, so very, very delicious on the scalding hot summer day. I watched an osprey flying and stared out in the vaporous, energy-zapping heat. This was the end of the second part of my hike up the Boise River to its headwaters, and I hoped that walking might become easier as I moved upstream. It had taken me four times as long to make it from the Snake River than I'd anticipated, and I still had two long segments to walk.

---

## THE PEOPLE'S STRETCH

*Part 3: From the City of Boise to Lucky Peak
Reservoir on the Solstice and Beyond
Arrowrock Reservoir*

J ust northwest of downtown Boise, Garden City stretches linearly
beside the Boise River. Along this stretch of river, the area is alive
with people who walk, ride bikes, and skate on the Boise River
Greenbelt paths.

As I walked along the paved and tree-lined path, swarms of
people around me were enjoying the summer weather. At a well-
known recreational river wave within the newly developed Whitewater
Park, a woman surfed with grace. Just below the wave, the 55-acre
Esther Simplot Park had come to life, with a fishing pond and popular
riding and hiking trails. This magical stretch along the river also
supports a wide variety of wildlife.

Garden City, where I live, is truly an oddity—a city within a city
(Boise). It is a place of trailer homes and renters, upscale homes,
and apartments, with at least five wineries and four breweries, and

the Riverside Hotel that brings in great music and a fine riverside restaurant. Telaya Winery has a grassy spread right on the river, and I sometimes hang out there and drink their nearly perfect Petit Verdot.

Just past the park, I arrived at 34th Street Market. Garden City resident Hannah Ball had the perfect pedigree for a gal who grew up here. Raised in a trailer park, she came to loathe that existence and became a developer of a different stripe. She was the inspiration for this place, where a weekly farmer's market draws hundreds of people to eat, drink, listen to music, and shop for produce and handmade crafts. Though she originally touted her development plan as emphasizing "local flavor," her business partner sold much of the local land to businesses with out-of-state interests and profit on their minds. Nevertheless, Hannah remains positive about what Garden City can accomplish for its residents and the surrounding city of Boise.

I continued walking south along the paved and crowded greenbelt, which silently merges with Boise. People were running, biking, and drinking at venues along the pathway, while others rafted down the river, swam, and sunbathed.

I came to a large rock, almost a boulder, beside an unnamed pond, inscribed with the words, "Celebrating the life of Cal Osburn." I did a double-take and reread it, because Cal Osburn was a friend of mine, a jovial man and father of John Osburn, who I've worked with for years as a conservationist. Cal always struck me as a happy guy, like Mr. Rogers on TV, a lover of nature and of people.

I had seen Cal the past autumn at a festival in Julia Davis Park, upstream from where I stood. But he didn't look well then and he was very thin. When he saw me, he took one of his trademark amusing cards from his wallet and put it in my hand. We smiled at one another, and I said "Thanks," before we shook hands. "Take care, Cal, I'll see you." But because he was obviously very ill, I didn't really think I would see him again.

*Surfing in Idaho.*

Cal carried an odd beauty, a joie de vivre, and held onto it till the last. His son quoted simply from his father: "To get along anywhere in this world, have a smile on your face, and good manners." I saw several other memorial markers on the walk upstream, and they made me think about living, and dying, well. It seems that there is a skill to dying well, and I think it reflects the way in which you live.

Memories helped create the "Ribbon of Jewels," a group of 12 parks and wildlife preserves located along a 20-mile stretch of the upper Boise River Greenbelt in the city of Boise, each named in honor of a prominent woman who donated her time, money, and energy to the Boise community. Along with parks and wildlife sanctuaries are a municipal golf course, the Idaho Fish and Game Morrison-Knudsen Nature Center, Boise State University, and a 36,000-acre Boise River Wildlife Management Area that skirts Lucky Peak Reservoir to support deer and elk wintering range.

I call this stretch of the river "the people's stretch," because plenty of people enjoy these places. Consider, for example, the man who had taken his daughter fishing for crayfish. When I met them, they'd caught three little crayfish in a big ol' bucket, but there was promise of more as they ran from hole to hot spot in search of the tasty miniature lobsters in the river. Or a young couple, clearly in love, who posed with a puny fish they'd caught. Another couple, celebrating their sixteenth anniversary with great joy, posed for a picture. All of them seemed to be enjoying the present.

As I walked on, I overheard a passel of kids who were walking along in the heat of the day. One of them said, "This guy started out barefooted and with long hair this morning." His friends listened casually until he stopped on the path to gain their full attention. "So, guess how'd he ended up?" Of course, one of the kids had to take the bait—there's one in every crowd—"I don't know, what happened to him?" "He got wise and went home with long hair and barefooted." There was general groaning and punching afterward. Even a duck looked up! I thought that Cal Osborn would've loved that silliness.

I continued upstream until I reached the Bethine Church River Trail, one of the jewels in the Boise ribbon. This 24-acre natural area creates a tranquil place for visitors and a quiet respite in the heart

Rafters arrive at the end of their float at Ann Morrison Park.

of the city. It supports riparian habitat, wildlife nesting places, and ponds and a stream for fish. It was a chirpy place that day, filled with bird life, and I thought it was a nice place to remember Bethine, the wife of Idaho Senator Frank Church, who gave many wonderful gifts to Idahoans and helped create the Sawtooth Society, a nonprofit that provides funds to protect the magnificent Sawtooth National Recreation Area in Central Idaho.

Beyond Bethine's trail, I passed through Barber Park, a grassy space for the 125,000 people who raft the river annually, and another piece of land above the marshy land of Barber Park, which is undeveloped and lesser known, beneath the bridge on Idaho Route 21. Beyond that, and nearly within sight, were the Boise River Diversion Dam and Lucky Peak.

## Up to Lucky Peak—lucky me!

The largest diversion of water on the Boise River is located 7 miles southeast of the city, where the Boise River Diversion Dam fills the New York Canal, part of the New York Irrigation District, a network of canals built by the Bureau of Reclamation and controlled by various irrigation districts throughout Southeast Idaho. That canal was many hard years in the making and today creates the most important human-constructed watercourse in Boise and beyond. It delivers water to businesses and residents and provides water to crops and wildlife downstream. The canal takes a sizeable portion (42,815 cubic feet per second is the maximum amount of water it can carry) out of the river and carries it 20 miles west, losing water along the way to smaller canals that irrigate the landscape along its path, eventually to Lake Lowell, which empties into a complex series of drains and canals and occasionally flows as far as the Lower Boise or Snake Rivers.

As I crossed the New York Canal, a stout man in a pickup truck confronted me.

"What are you doing here?" he asked. I assume that he was a watermaster who controlled the flow of water, protected the canal, and tried to keep people from drowning in its fast-flowing water.

"I'm hiking up the river."

"You can't go this way."

"Oh, I see," I said. We stared at each blankly for about 10 seconds.

"You'll have to go back," he said.

"OK. But I'd like to go forward if you'll let me."

"I'm sorry. I can't. I could give you a ride out if you'd like."

"No thanks, I'll walk if that's alright."

Then I asked whether the canal was funded by the U.S. government, and didn't that allow me to trespass on it, but I received no answer. When he asked if I'd seen the "No Trespassing!" signs and locks on the gate, he received silence from me. It was nice that we understood each other like that, but neither of us made a believer of the other. He had his job, but I had mine too.

So I turned around and walked 3 miles out to avoid further confrontation and took the beautiful Oregon Trail through the sagebrush instead. This tiny stretch I was walking on was part of the 2,170-mile route followed by thousands of settlers who traveled west from Missouri to Oregon in the mid- to late 1800s. That day's trail, however, went around a subdivision that I didn't want to pass through, so I found a bike path beside the river—a long, shadeless, and solitary path on this heated summer solstice day—and headed upstream toward Lucky Peak Dam.

When I finally climbed up beside the dam, where it connected into solid rock on one side of the canyon, I was impressed by the dam's massive size. It seemed engineered to maximize the size of the reservoir per cubic foot of concrete poured. It required a monumental undertaking of human effort in the 1950s. As I walked along the top of the dam, I could see that the reservoir below was full of activity: the hustle-bustle of people scurrying around the water and having fun. Swimming trunks and bikinis were much in vogue. A pair of sailboats was anchored, sailors baking on their decks. I smiled at what the reservoir offered to people from Boise. Then I veered off and down to trace the reservoir's steep banks. It was easy at first, as I walked on a dirt road, but then it became ever less so as the path disappeared and the steep hillside fell away into the water.

I walked for miles along the sloping banks of the reservoir. Once in awhile, I'd come upon people camping, who seemed startled by

*The Boise River and the New York Canal, which diverts roughly half of the river for agriculture and wildlife.*

the fact of my walking in the blasting heat amid the desolation of the sagebrush nothingness from which I'd come. I walked several miles along the unroaded portion of the sprawling reservoir until I began to feel woozy, incoherent, invisible—a ghost skimming along like mist flowing in waves across the water.

Around a bend, I saw some sort of mirage: a couple and two children who all seemed to be steaming under glass beside their boat on a dock in the middle of the Sahara. It beat watching TV, I guess, but this did seem a curious form of recreation. I was, of course, hiking on the barren slope of a drowned canyon, and that seemed somehow equally absurd. Each member of the family was eating a sloppy sandwich. Both children looked bored, as one wiped mayonnaise from the corner of his mouth. I could see boats pulling skiers farther out, the wakes of the boats and skis forming geometric patterns that flowed through the water on waves moving shoreward, crashing ashore in tidy lines. *Swish, kahoossh, swish, swish*, the sounds came.

"Hello!" I called. They all turned around and looked surprised.

"Hi!" the man said. "What are you doing?"

"I'm out for a walk."

"Do you need something to eat or drink?"

"No, I'm fine. What are you doing?" The children looked at me as if I were an alien on a trip from the Nebula Digitalis, or from the drug underworld.

"We're just having lunch," the man said, as they continued eating. "You look hot."

I waited a few seconds and formed an idea. "Hey, I've got something for you." I had earlier picked up a discarded antler just for something to carry. It felt good in my hands.

"What is it?" his wife said, protectively.

"Oh, it's just something I found on my walk. It's an antler. I thought your kids might like it."

"Sure," her husband said, skeptically.

The children looked expectedly to see what it was and if they might have it. At least that's what I saw in their eyes. I walked down to the dock and extended the antler to the father to give to his kids, but I dropped it into the mud. I stooped down to pick it up and gave it to the young boy who was most curious about this antler-thing. I didn't want to be perceived as a threat to any of the family so I backed away. "You've got to share it with your sister." The boy wasn't sure what to say to this odd alien.

"Did you just find this?" he asked.

"Yeah, over there." I pointed back to where I had come from, and then I figured I should leave about now. "A big buck left it behind a while ago. He didn't need it any more."

"You think I could find the buck?" This boy was an optimist!

"Nah, I doubt it. I think he's long gone. But you two can have this one." Yeah, it was definitely time for me to go; his mom frowned and dad smiled. "Hey, I'll see you guys!"

"Do you need a ride somewhere?" Dad asked.

"No thanks. I'll just walk." But as I looked along the shore, I wasn't sure that was the best decision.

I walked several more miles through the intense heat of the day along the reservoir, back to Highway 21, and then I hitchhiked downriver to my truck and drove home to sleep on this longest day of the year.

## Along the hot hellhole of Arrowrock Reservoir

When I next had a chance to hike around Arrowrock Reservoir, which is adjacent to the upper portion of Lucky Peak Reservoir, nearly a month had passed. I dreaded the thought of hiking along this open route and delayed doing it until late July, after the water level in the reservoir had dropped significantly. The day was as hot as sizzling bacon.

The Lucky Peak Reservoir is shaped like an arrowhead on the map, where the South Fork and Middle Fork of the Boise River meet. The Arrowrock Dam, further upstream, was completed in 1915 by the Army Corps of Engineers and the Bureau of Reclamation to provide irrigation for hundreds of thousands of acres of farmland. In its day, this reservoir was the biggest one ever made and was a showcase for the Corps. The reservoir's water capacity was 227,224 acre-feet in 1997, but the original capacity was estimated at 291,600 acre-feet. The difference is attributed to sediment collection in the reservoir— and that 64,376 acre-feet amounts to quite a bit of displaced water.

Arrowrock Dam is operated to provide a full Lucky Peak Reservoir downstream until Labor Day, so it is severely drained, or drafted to regulate the conditions of Lucky Peak Reservoir for recreation. That priority leaves Arrowrock a poor candidate to maintain fish and wildlife habitat, recreation values, or sediment control. By 1997, Arrowrock had lost nearly 7 percent of its capacity to sedimentation, according to a Bureau of Reclamation study that year. The reservoir had not been "sluiced" to remove the collected sediment since the construction of the Lucky Peak Dam in the mid-1950s.

Presumably, the sluice gates have been closed since 1954, and the sediment acquired accounts for its lowered capacity for water. The obvious problem is how to pass the sediment from Arrowrock and not fill Lucky Peak Reservoir or affect downriver irrigators and the floodplain around Boise. In 2014, the proposed solution was to enlarge the reservoir, but that proved far too expensive and the problem has continued to grow.

*The beautiful devastation that occurs annually when Arrowrock Reservoir is lowered to provide water for Lucky Peak Reservoir.*

Another problem that the Bureau and Corps have encountered is the existence of bull trout, a sensitive species under the Endangered Species Act, in both Lucky Peak and Arrowrock Reservoirs. Bull trout require low-temperature water to survive. They were originally a migratory species and depended greatly on the once vast salmon runs to provide their food, as salmon die after spawning. But the salmon aren't here anymore, because they cannot migrate through downstream dams, so the bulls are stuck and are relatively stunted until the dams come down. Until then, federal agencies must help the bull trout survive and thrive. This management effort will likely help the fish survive in the reservoirs, but the bulls will fare better in the upper, wilder, and lesser-touched parts of the Boise River drainage.

The road that runs along the shore of Arrowrock is poorly maintained and provides a jaw-jarring washboard experience throughout summer, making the route difficult to enjoy for any purpose. It also made for a miserable hike. There are few places to launch a boat in Arrowrock Reservoir, which is a dreadful and beautiful place.

Twenty years ago, the Corps of Engineers launched a proposal to build a dam at Twin Springs on the Middle Fork of the Boise River. Citizens generated plenty of opposition and outrage about that dam, both in Idaho and nationally, and as a result, the Corps chose not to build the dam.

That was a big win for Idaho Rivers United, which advocated protecting the river from being inundated. Killing the Twin Springs Dam had followed many wins for irrigators and developers. Diversion Dam (completed in 1909), Arrowrock Dam (1915), Anderson Ranch Reservoir (1950), and Lucky Peak Dam (1955) were all completed to provide flood control, irrigation, eventually electrical power, and recreation to boost revenues.

In the end, the Boise River was controlled, and spring and early summer flooding would be limited. Or so it was said. These were popular projects in the first half of the 1900s when most people cheered the greatness of the growing dam-building technology. But eventually the tide turned when people saw the downside of the dams, and Idaho Rivers United capitalized on the public consensus.

Water is in greater demand today than it was in the last century, thanks to the growing population and encroaching development in the Treasure Valley. Increasing the volume of Arrowrock Dam would have served irrigators for additional water and for fewer damaging floods. It would also benefit the increased population in the Lower Boise River drainage and developers of housing projects, which demand, and get, their rights to develop. But at $1.26 billion, increasing Arrowrock's volume was deemed too expensive. Moreover, the Anderson Ranch Reservoir, which was assessed for expansion in 2019, would yield 29,000 additional acre-feet of water for $31 million and therefore was deemed more likely for reconstruction. Compare that to the 64,376 acre-feet that would be restored in Arrowrock if it were again sluiced.

As I wound down my day of hiking, I vowed to return another time to finish the hike from Atlanta to Spangle Lake in the Sawtooth Mountains. And soaking in the hot springs by Ninemeyer Campground in Atlanta was a perfectly fine way to end another grueling day of hiking.

*An emerald pool in the upper Middle Fork of the Boise River.*

# UP TO THE WILDERNESS!

## *Part 4: Hiking from Atlanta to Spangle Lake in the Sawtooth Wilderness*

I *can't believe I forgot to bring my sleeping bag*. Today, I'd planned to start a 16-mile hike from Atlanta, Idaho, to the ultimate headwaters of the Middle Fork of the Boise River at Spangle Lake, in the highest country of the Sawtooth Wilderness. This day marks the beginning of the final stretch of my hike from the Snake River to the top of the Boise River drainage, on the Middle Fork of the Boise River. But I need a decent sleeping bag, like the one I left at home.

Spangle Lake will sparkle, glitter, and gleam! I just know it. It's an exotic place in my mind right now, so far away from the urban scene in Boise. Earlier today, I tried, unsuccessfully, to find a weather report on my truck radio to determine whether the temperature would be too cold for me to go on up to the lake without a sleeping bag. And my cellphone had no reception. And the weather looked stormy. Here I am, sitting on the tailgate of my pickup, drinking another afternoon

beer on this gorgeous and cool, late-summer day, feeling cranky about forgetting something as important as my sleeping bag. *Can I do the trip without a sleeping bag?*

Cursing myself, once again, for forgetting to bring the bag, I contemplate going back to Boise to retrieve it—down the Atlanta Road (bumpity-goddamned-bumpity-bump, all the stinkin' way), past Queens River, downriver to Dutch Creek Station, on a shortcut to the North Fork (oh, that would be pretty ... for the fourth freaking time), up and over to Idaho City (through all of the cheerless mining tailings), down to Lucky Peak Reservoir (the grand apotheosis of I-don't-know-what, maybe the unflooded city of Boise?). At least I would miss Arrowrock Reservoir on the way down, and that would be some consolation. *Nah. Not going back. I don't want to go back to town. I want to hike in the wilderness today.* So I drink another beer, trying to gain some sort of lousy consolation.

When three young guys pull up in a carryall rig and start to unload their backpacks, I watch them and ponder what I'm going to do. Cheer and energy are on their side, but not mine. I drink from the bottle and pull out some raisins and peanuts, chewing and listening to Frank Sinatra crooning on my truck's CD player.

As they unload gear, we exchange pleasant salutations and talk about their plans to work on the trail up ahead in the Sawtooth Wilderness. They tell me they're paid by a consultant who contracts with the U.S. Forest Service, similar to what the old Civilian Conservation Corps had done more than 85 years ago (and similar to what President Joe Biden recently proposed in his list of proclamations in 2021). The CCC was a federally funded program, part of the New Deal enacted by President Franklin Roosevelt during the Great Depression. The program hired young, unemployed people to create many of the superb trails in the Sawtooth National Forest and other forests within and outside of Idaho. The CCC's legacy lives on in the current funding of Forest Service trail projects.

I mutter to myself (but loud enough for them to hear), "I can't believe that I forgot to bring my most excellent, new, down sleeping bag." Then, after trying to take another swig from an empty bottle, I throw it despairingly in the back of my pickup.

"Oh, that's pretty bad," one of the guys says. They laugh a little as two of them don their packs. "You ever backpacked before?"

I shrug and grimace. "Hey, you guys want a beer? You old enough to drink?" They snicker but refuse my offer. One of the guys places a sleeping bag on the tailgate beside me, says he doesn't think that his dog will miss it. His dog's sleeping bag. "Just leave it in the truck when you return," he says.

"Hey, thanks!" I say brightly, abandoning all pride. I listen to Sinatra singing "That's Life." Right. We all live that way sometimes. I reach for another bottle in the back of my truck, but as I walk around to the driver's seat, I notice a perilously low tire. I close my eyes for a second and inhale deeply. *Screw it! I'll fix it on my way out.* I'll leave the truck behind and hike away from its annoying problems. I pour the other half of the beer into the dirt, pull on my pack, and head out behind those young guys, my saviors.

## Into the wilderness

The men have launched quickly down the trail, and I don't think I'll see them again. But about 2 miles up, there they are, smoking a bowl at the entry point to the Sawtooth Wilderness. I say, "Hey," trying to sound enormously cool, and chat with them a bit. They tell me that their goal for the day is Plummer Peak, a nearly 10,000-foot peak that's roughly 15 miles up the trail—farther than I planned to walk

today. The altitude where we began the trip was 5,400 feet, and it was already four o'clock.

"That's ambitious!" But I really want to say, *That's impossible*. "Good luck." I sign into the hiker ledger and walk by. Soon they pass me, but their dog hangs back to bark ferociously, apparently wanting to regain his sleeping bag. "You lose, Buckwheat!" I whispered. "It's all mine now!" He shows me his teeth. "It's going to be a trip like that, is it?"

After about 5 miles, I stop by a grove of turning aspen and Douglas fir trees, which make an otherwise parched spot shady and cool.

The nearby river now flows the width of a softball pitch, and it has the personality of a chatty creek. Its banks are granite, and they squeeze water into a serpentine-green slide. The river begs me to stop. So I stop. It begs me to fish. So I fish. The river is as productive as it is beautiful, and I keep three small trout. Then, among the trees, not far from the river, I set up my tent and throw my gear inside. *This is a very fine spot to be camping*.

Though the too-short sleeping bag smells like wet dog, the sudden pitter-pat of rain on the tent lulls me to sleep. The smell, however, soon leads me into half-waking dreams of a dog howling at my feet and grabbing them in its mouth with a growl.

In the morning, I cook a trout breakfast and dry out the tent a bit. Looking up, I see a smoky sky masking 9,900 foot Mattingly Peak in wisps of rising, gauzy clouds. But beyond Mattingly, Spangle Lake still beckons, and I pack my gear once again and head out.

This stretch of river reminds me that the Boise River still retains its soul, which had seemed lost when I walked around the still waters in its reservoirs earlier in the year. As I struggled along the unkempt trails not far from its confluence with the Snake, the Boise River seemed to cast a mysterious, dark, and industrial truth about what had been done to it. The river ages and grows wiser and wider as it flows downhill, like an old woman who has grown crusty and cranky, and who isn't going to tolerate the bullshit she faced in her youth, ever again. But the river knows who she is and flows on and on, regardless.

*A sego lily.*

The river's character changes in each incarnation, but always, always, it keeps its soul, though perhaps hidden, like a person facing difficult times who chooses to move forward in the face of constant challenges. The river remains stalwart as it flows on. What else can it do but move on?

Here in the wilderness, it flows wildly, cascading out of the high mountains. As I reach a meadow, it slows, and columbines and chokecherries grow along the path as the drainage ripens with the changing colors of autumn. Beavers have been here recently and may come again. Deer, bear, elk, wolves, wolverine are out there somewhere in these kind woods, but I haven't seen a single one of them. Not yet, anyway.

△△△

*Now I need to let you in on a secret. I have to make a second confession, to bring this trip into proper perspective: I also forgot my knife. I know, I know, you're asking, "Your sleeping bag **and** your* knife? Uh, Mike, did you remember your stove, your underpants, socks, food, and your jacket?" I proudly say "yes" to those, and anyway, I didn't necessarily need underpants, did I? You ask, "How did you clean the fish and cut the rope to set up that tent, the one that you probably forgot?" Well, you already know that I didn't forget my tent, right?

I searched through my backpack for a knife and then searched for inspiration. Nothing. I looked for sharp sticks, jagged rocks, arrowheads, and other more primitive tools lying about that would enable me to perform tasks like gutting a fish. Not a truly sharp thing came to mind or hand so I growled and went out fishing and thought, something will rise! And, yes, indeed, as I already mentioned, the fish did.

I had three fish to clean—a decent meal, right? Maybe. But there was nothing to clean them with. So I went through my backpack again, looking for something that might slice the fish from asshole to gills without ripping them apart: Corkscrew? Naw. Bottle opener? Fork? Too messy. Fishhooks? Possible in a pinch. Fingers, pencil, pen? Ick, no way, what a mess!

Ah-hah! I found my first aid kit. Maybe a razor blade? Noooo. Rock, paper, scissors? Ah, yes, there are scissors in the kit. They would cut bandages—or fish and rope. Perfect. It felt good to be back in the 21st century once again, where scissors could beat rocks as a tool. I made a note to myself: Make a list of things to bring on every backpacking trip that might be helpful. Think of TP, for instance. And please remember to refill the fuel container once in a while. Bring matches too. On other solo trips I had forgotten each of these. I might bring some companions as well next time.

△△△

## Mountains of gold

A red-tailed hawk screams at me from her perch. "Shaddup, smarty wings," I answer. She needs none of the creature comforts that I need. I soldier on and think about yesterday's drive to Atlanta. I saw mines and landslides and buildings and forest fire scars. The land is changing, the town is changing, but the river endures. It cleans up every mess, given time.

Mines and mining surround the community of Atlanta. Naked rocks are stacked in piles, defining the placer mining that occurred in years past. Roads climb up every tributary in Atlanta to other mines, primarily gold and silver mines. The Atlanta Gold company still mines the valuable minerals, but faced with lawsuits from the Idaho Conservation League and others, the company hasn't produced high quantities of gold in recent years.

Small-time miners scour streams for gold, and in the process make a mess of fish habitat—not habitat for steelhead or salmon or lamprey, though, because those fish were eliminated years ago by dams on the Snake River. The future of mining in Atlanta will depend upon the price of gold, silver, and molybdenum and the price of cleaning up the old mines, like the Tolache, the Minerva, and the Monarch. Future mining will mostly depend on the price of that most useless of elements: gold. I mean, really, what do you do with gold that can't be done without it?

*Spangle Lake.*

And consider the desire, the motivation, and the conniving politics required to get to it. Don't get me started.

△△△

As I hike through the wilderness, change is occurring everywhere: the leaves fall from aspens, the river's flow grows less forceful, the air feels cooler. Somehow beauty grows. It's good to hike a nice trail and good to catch fish. I feel good here, above the mines and human manipulations of the land. Of course, I remember that the trail must be constructed and maintained by people, and people must transplant fish to the river and to alpine lakes. There's joy in carrying my many gizmos and maps purchased from REI. And coffee. Ah yes, coffee from Costa Rica or Kona or Kenya, heated up on my metallic stove fueled by gasoline: these have all come from other places. My boots were crafted in China, my backpack and aluminum pans came from some faraway, unknown place. All of these human trappings are loaded in the pack I'm carrying on my back. I realize that I can't get away from production, consumption, and practicality, but here in the wilderness, they feel less obtrusive and outrageous as I futilely deny their importance.

## Spangle Lake beckons

The mountains and streams, trees and wildlife feel eternal, the place sublime and golden. Hiking gives me time to think about what the world is doing to us and we to it: pollution, population growth, fighting for things (fighting, always fighting, always), wanting all of life's pleasures, seeking immortality in the clouds. But when I look around, I see beauty right here—a Shangri-La, a worldly paradise away from the hassles of modern life, a gift to all who take the trouble to see, enjoy, and preserve it.

*Spangle Lake with the mountains behind.*

It's late afternoon, and I've arrived at Spangle Lake. Camping in the most perfect campsite, I find my hiking and working friends and their dog. Their presence is marked only by the absence of impacts of other people—an absence that seems present, because the three men have cleaned up all the other the campsites. I hoot "hello" and begin searching for the second-best campsite. I don't find that campsite, but I do find a nice place above the lake. I know I can catch another few fish here and watch the lake darken into night.

Spangle Lake delivers what I had hoped for—fish, solitude, fine scenery, reflection, and a natural place to sit and read and write. The lake is alive with sparkles, sparks, and flashing specks of light: it is beautiful. I guess that is all I really want: a way to look at our world that pleases. This whole damned world is topsy-turvy—but I think it might be alright. I fall asleep.

Day three. I catch a 20-inch cutthroat in a nearby lake. She stays still for me long enough to take a picture before she swishes her tail and swims away in the shallow water. Her girth is greater than my grip. She would have been a prize at dinnertime! I feel a fool for letting her go, but I also feel superior for letting her go.

## Spangling dreams

As I continue my journey at the top of the world, I come to a place where a line of dead whitebark pines spreads across a ridge. They are like a line of grave markers, and I lament their deaths. These pines lived for so many years—hundreds at least, maybe a thousand—and through so much brutal weather that their twisted forms define their lives. Wind and deep snow have bent them, and they adapted by growing low. Others have branched on only one side of their trunk. A few are stout and straight-growing and seem to have lived most fully, sheltered in place, protected by boulders, where the vicissitudes of fate deposited them on a warm and protected spot in this otherwise harsh environment. Still, drought or disease, or both, brought them death long ago. They had been lucky, though.

*A whitebark pine seedling.*

Another few trees seem to be taking their last breath of $CO_2$, with stories of their lives contained in thin strips of bark, winding up their trunks like barber poles. As I walk over the ridge, I see a remarkable thing: seedlings of whitebark pines are growing, a new generation is jumping up from the rocky soil with the pure luck of happenstance and the hope for success firmly on their side. They are young, though, and don't know what they will face.

When I return to Spangle Lake, as I again cast my line into the water, I see a pair of ospreys flying above me. Foolishly, I try to coax them closer, holding up the first fish I catch. "See what you're missing?" I tell them, as I release the hapless fish into the lake.

Quickly, the birds are far away, soaring in a spiral updraft and headed out beyond the next ridge. It must be nice to see the world from an osprey's eye!

My climbing these past few days has seemed so endless—my path going up and up and relentlessly up. The ospreys' climb seems effortless, and their flight looks fun. I have a notion, though, that climbing in the air may be just as tough as climbing a mountain—but in theory, catching a ride on a thermal sounds good.

Now that the trail crew has moved on, I move my camp to their empty campsite for my last night. From here, the view is stupendous. A view this good is incomparable. I sleep like a ton of bricks.

Another fine morning, I drink my coffee and enjoy a trout breakfast. As I begin walking on a smooth downhill run, I pass the columbine again in the cool, moist forest, and the "V" of the river course.

*Three men who were clearing trails within the Sawtooth Wilderness—and their dog who snuck into the picture.*

I hope that maybe, just maybe, my working friends have already cleared the broken, tangled trees and those nasty, thorny blackberry vines on the trail up ahead. Or perhaps, by now, they have walked back to where my truck is parked, pulled off the flat tire, and replaced it with a new one. If wishes were ospreys, hikers could fly! When I find them and their nifty dog on the way down, I realize that the men have worked hard to clear the avalanche path ahead of me—and even the dog is nice.

Finally, back at my truck, I replace the tire and begin the long drive home. The road unwinds before me, as I return to civilization— back to my home in calm, happy, beautiful, and metropolitan Boise, the city that is defined by the remarkable Boise River. We are thieves of the river's energy! I will remember sparkling light on Spangle Lake and will dream that everything will turn out as perfectly along the Boise River as a picture postcard of a wilderness reflection.

176

# FLIGHT

It was before dawn, and a circle occurred around the moon as tiny ice crystals fell on my face, like gentle rain. I received a call from the nurse who helped care for my mom, Marjorie Fassler Medberry, at the care home near my house in Boise, Idaho. Mom's time was near, she said. I told her I'd be there in a few minutes. The coming of death is simple like that. It is intuitive, a foreboding feeling.

Wiping the chill from my eyes, I stared at the moon for a moment in the early morning light, then hurried to get out of the house with a warm jacket and a book to read. As I walked, I thought about who my mother might have been and disappeared in thought.

△△△

When I was a child of 10, I was messing around on the sidewalk in front of our house in the Mantua Hills subdivision in Fairfax, Virginia, rubbing the ends of popsicle sticks on the curb, when Mom came outside. She told me she would be gone for a while and would bring back groceries. She swiftly got into her new Chevrolet as I continued sharpening the sticks. She flew away from the curb in that ivory, 1966 Super Sport Impala, as if she were being chased by death, throwing slush and gravel over the wide sidewalk. The sounds of firecrackers and cherry-bombs blasted when she stomped on the accelerator. What was *that* about?

But I remember it well. It was a distinctive moment. My dad, Ray, was gone on an Air Force junket. I had been down that road to the grocery store about a million times, beside Accotink Creek, skittering on my steel-wheeled skateboard, gliding like an uncontrolled rocket, with every little pebble stunning my legs as I went down Rocky Mountain Road, up Mantua Road, and then rode an enormously long way through the cold forest over to the Fairfax Circle. I imagined where my mom was headed. She seemed to be escaping something, not just going for groceries.

Mom returned within an hour and told me what happened as I stood on the sidewalk. I must've looked cold and a bit confused. The exact words have been long lost, but the memory of her expression remains clear as she knelt down and

*Pictured Left: Marj in a publicity photo from the 1940s.*

pressed her hands to my cheeks. She spoke softly, whispered. She said, "You know the route, son." I figured she was headed for a little excitement outside of our boring residential subdivision. I understood that—I was bored of the popsicle sticks too. I imagined making a small cage for an astronaut-mouse and sending it up to the moon under a helium balloon.

This time, she said, she was foiled by a black-and-white car with a cherry on top. Its light whirled, its tires chattered, and its siren wailed as the police car emerged from an invisible gravel patch beside the road. That cherry beacon turned the road into a bright aurora of red and yellow as the cop gave chase. After he pulled over her galloping Impala, he took his sweet, damned time, sitting in his car before slowly walking over to the Impala's driver's side.

She said he was tense as he pulled out a book of tear-off tickets and began writing. He told her she was doing 75 in a 45 zone. Mom had apologized. I imagined her voice, a voice I'd heard all my life that was as sweet and complex as tupelo honey that hid her damped-down emotions.

The cop lopped the ticket out of his book and handed it to her. He'd given her the maximum fine. I imagined her gripping the steering wheel with stiffened arms, as she thanked him. It was an embarrassing speeding ticket for her, because the Impala was the first car that my dad bought for her, and she had just received her new driver's license.

That was 1966, the year of the great blizzard in Washington, D.C., when 2 feet of snow fell on the city. It was very quiet in Fairfax, and the turnpike held only a skiff of snow. She said nothing for a time, stewed, and stared out beyond the road.

In the silence, I imagined tall trees blurring along the two-lane road with stinky little Accotink Creek running beside it. Snow fell on dead leaves of dogwood and maple trees and, I imagined, blocked her view around each curve. Even now, I can smell the sharp redolence of Accotink Creek: sassafras, cinnamon, beer, and the reek of outhouses. Box turtles and black snakes moved through the grasses in the deciduous forest and lamprey eels slipped up the creek and that reeking smell of pollution tore at your nose. We kids named the creek "Aqua-stink Creek." Mom told us never to go there: there were weirdos lurking around and the water held the chance of being diseased. She once told me she had been raped, though she never mentioned when or where. Regardless, I didn't know what that meant back in those days, and we kids had gone down to Aqua-stink Creek on our own to capture box turtles, black snakes, or lampreys and claim them as our pets. The emotion that was in the drive that Mom had taken down toward Fairfax Circle—even now, after half a century, that moment remains in my mind.

△△△

As I walked toward the rest home to see my old and dying mother, I imagined what my young mother had done to leave Galt and move to San Francisco in the 1940s, the war years. We had talked about her growing up as I grew up, and I realized that she had a natural ability to size-up people and see through to the heart of any character. She also had a mistrust for Galt. Long ago, she told me about how she had confronted her mother.

"Marjie, where do you think you're going?" Elma, her mother, asked. Marjorie had a knapsack over her shoulder, looking at her mom on their porch in Galt.

"I want to see San Francisco again," she spoke decisively. "I've graduated from high school and it's time for me to move on." Her best friend, Virginia, had suggested a trip somewhere beyond the farm, somewhere bright and new, somewhere beyond the dusty rainbow of their dour lives, where they could fly. They had talked about going to the city and other, more exotic parts of the world when they were in high school, and now that both of them had graduated, Marjie was all packed up to travel with Virginia. "Right now, Mom," she said.

"You've got your chores to do first, Marjie." Elma spoke without looking up.

"Mom, I've done them. I've fed the chickens, milked the cow, and slopped pigs like I've done every day for 10 years. I'm sick of it to here," she said, swiping a finger across her throat, "and I'm sick of this place." She was triggered by her mother's blasé response but also by something else. "I hate this place! It's such a dirt patch. You and Dad can hardly afford to pay for food and we barely make ends meet." She was on a roll. "It's feast or famine and one fewer mouth to feed will lighten the load. Jack is gone to Sacramento and Herb is building the Alcan Highway to Alaska. DeeDee is under your skirt and

Douglas is, well, he's only a baby. So I'm heading to San Francisco to Emperor Norton's palace." She didn't want to tell her mom where else she would go, so Emperor Norton's villa would suffice.

Elma squinted at her daughter. "Don't get your damned bowels in an uproar, Marjie." Her mother looked fierce with a pair of headless chickens in one hand and, as Mom told it, a cleaver in the other. She held up the dead chickens for her daughter to see. She needed the help. "You got work to do!"

Oh, did Marjie ever want out of that tarnished landscape! She'd read about Joshua Abraham Norton, known as Emperor Norton, in the high school library in Galt, and he caught her attention. He was all the rage in the mid-19th century, during the Gilded Age, when the wealth of robber-baron industrialists like the Vanderbilts and Carnegies stood in stark comparison to the poverty-stricken riff-raff of financial misfortune, like the Fasslers. Emperor Norton was San Francisco's imperious oddball, and in 1859 he proclaimed himself, in the *San Francisco Evening Bulletin* newspaper, "Norton I, Emperor of the United States." He was bold and insistent and commanded that all representatives from the United States come to San Francisco to address the coming Civil War. The Emperor lived in the seaside quarter of San Francisco, and when he went out to wander the streets of the city, he wore a military uniform with epaulettes hanging from his shoulders, ostrich feathers sticking out of his frontiersman's hat, and a military sword clamped to his hip, ready to enforce all of his demands. He was an odd but harmless mascot for the people of San Francisco, and they loved his eccentricities. Mom liked Emperor Norton I, as he defined a nonconformist and railed against the industrialists. He also proclaimed a $25 fine for using the name "Frisco" for the city of San Francisco, but Mom used the term for color and defiance.

Mom wrote a letter to her old friends, who had been neighbors of her parents in San Francisco, when the Fasslers lived at 766 Sutter Street, and she planned to head to their place when she arrived. She wasn't planning on compromising one bit, and she was going to hilly Frisco, the city of clean, pressed-white, and perfectly wonderful sailors. San Francisco had that shiny, three-year-old Golden Gate Bridge, which she longed to see and to walk upon. Everyone talked about San Francisco and its bridge, even in Galt. The war had just begun, the Depression would soon be over, and there were jobs, jobs, and more jobs.

"Which sure as hell paid more than slopping the pigs," Mom told me, apropos of nothing I understood at age 10. The news of the war and war jobs in San Francisco was in all of the national papers, in *The Sacramento Union* and in the farm-town newspaper, *The Galt Herald*. Her life simply wouldn't wait any longer. But her friend Virginia's dreams would have to wait, because she got married on a whim, pregnant on a joy, and she never left Galt with Marjie for the city. Still, they were lifelong friends.

"We've been through all of this, Marjie," Elma stared at her daughter. "You're needed here."

"Not enough, Mom. Not much. It's hard here. I've done a lot in Galt and Galt is no...." She remembered the overcrowded house and the bull that stalked her. She checked herself. "I'm just planning to visit, and I've earned the bus fare. I am going, Mom." Good God, Marjie thought. Her mom is so incredibly tedious, melodramatic, and brutal.

"Well, I guess you're old enough to go by yourself at 17, but there has been no real Emperor in San Francisco, child!" Elma felt frustrated with her recalcitrant daughter and she would set her foot down right now. "What did your father say about your *big plan* to fly the coop?" She stood holding the chickens as if they were invisible, the cleaver a prop of authority.

"Dad said it made sense. I sent a letter to one of our old friends, you remember the Currys, in San Francisco, and his wife is expecting me."

"Oh, for God's sake. That sour man!"

△△△

On this cold morning, as I left my house to walk toward Mom's rest home in Boise, I saw a wild and weedy plant with small, brilliant yellow flowers, a slender composite that bloomed in November beside my house; it was, unaccountably, still in bloom three months later. When I looked at the flower, I thought of the months my mom had spent in the rest home. I felt discouraged, acknowledging that I could no longer meet her needs and retain full-time work at a pharmacy. She had survived well enough in her home, but she

*Mom in her house in 2016.*

needed groceries and her yard needed care. A few months before she left to move to the rest home, we had a necessary discussion.

"Mom. Mom! Can you hear me? I need the keys to your car," I had said. She watched a show on television, which was blaring at jet-takeoff-volume whenever I went to her home. I'd visited her regularly for three years from across town, and I had stayed at her place for a couple days this time. "Mom, you can't drive anymore," I yelled. I spoke loudly because she didn't want to pay for hearing aids. The lack of thyroxine in her body was affecting her judgment and health, and she refused to take medication to deal with it. The week before, she had fallen backward from a step and smacked her head on concrete. A month prior to that, she had been in a car accident. She chuckled when she told me that she had talked her way out of getting the blame for that fender-bender.

Remarkably, Mom had moved to Boise 18 years earlier when I had a severe and unaccountable stroke. She flew from Sacramento to the hospital in Pocatello where I was taken after she was called by a physician who told her of my nearly dying while hiking in Craters of the Moon National Monument. She came out on the next plane, fearing the worst for me, recalling what had happened to her husband many years earlier, when he had died of brain cancer and a stroke.

Before she moved to Idaho, Mom and I had not been on speaking terms for 20 years because of my using cocaine, which she learned about by reading a page in my journal. It was June of 1981, I was 25, finished with college, and living in McCall, a small mountain town in Idaho, where I'd found a nice piece of land in a place where I wanted to live forever. I had begun to build a house but ran out of money in the recession of 1982. Before leaving California, I had built two houses in Davis, and now I was eager to build the house that would be mine. That was my dream: to build my house stick-by-stick, brick-by-brick, and to live happily ever after with two kids and a lovely wife. But the market went bad that year and I had to borrow $10,000 from my mom to finish the house before winter clawed in, bringing −20° F temperatures and 6 feet of snow that year. She visited the next June, along with Dave, my good friend from Sacramento. At the end of her visit, I wrote in my journal the following entry:

Dave Martin and I had been fishing in Little Payette Lake. We had done fairly well and had an exceptional time talking and rowing and drinking beer. Both of us were in high spirits by the time we made it home. When I was in the kitchen and Dave was outside cleaning the fish, Mom came up to me and announced that she was leaving first thing in the morning. When I asked why, she replied that it was late now and Dave might be too tired for the drive.

"What?" I asked her at the time. "I thought you were going to leave on Wednesday." It was Saturday evening.

"Well," her voice quivered, "we were." She turned away from my bewildered stare. "I read in your journal about your taking cocaine every time I sent you money to work on the house." She threw that like boiling water in my face. She said that she had looked at my check deposit slips and the deposits of money she'd sent me and it coincided with the days of my using cocaine. I started to deny this but realized that she was probably right. I told her that I had paid for splurges of cocaine like they were bottles of champagne, and they held about as much punch as too many cups of coffee.

"So why did you have to use cocaine then?"

"Didn't have to, just did. We were tired and cocaine seemed like a reward for our hard work," I replied. Then again, it didn't take much coaxing after such a hard and productive day of work on the house to share a treat.

She got melodramatic, like the whole wide world was ending, and who cares anyway. I can't remember all that we said to one another, but one thing that she said was that this would all be over tomorrow, forgotten, and gone. She would survive, and so would I.

She and Dave left the next morning, and I received a short note from her the next week which said:

Dear Mike—Enclosed is some reading matter for you, if you have the time. Got it from my medical book.

Love, M.

It was a torn-out page from the *Merck Manual* on "Dependence of the Cocaine Type," which read, "Cocaine is the prototype of stimulant drugs that in high doses can provide euphoric excitement and, occasionally, hallucinatory experiences ... to which psychic dependence develops that can lead to addiction."

Two days later, I sent her the words from Crosby, Stills, Nash, and Young's song, "Teach Your Children," which I hoped would let her know that we had our differences but that I loved her anyway.

It was tit-for-tat between us, and neither budged for nearly 20 years afterward. It was very old news by the time I had my stroke, and she moved to Idaho to help me recover. I learned that my mother would always be my mother, and she would show compassion whether or not she felt I deserved it. It is that bond of mother to child, with both of us realizing that there were more important things than holding a tired, meaningless grudge. When she came to Boise, she gave me gentle and caring help.

△△△

Of course, each of us had strong opinions about the way the world should work, but when I took her keys, I was the one giving her practical advice. "Mom, you can't drive anymore." She had recovered quickly from her fall, and we had laughed—embarrassed—at the fender-bender.

"Like hell I can't drive!" she asserted, ever the contrarian.

I persevered. "Mom, the doctor said that you can hardly see. You had a wreck last month. Last week you fell and hit your head. Mother, it's time."

She tightened her lips and looked annoyed as she walked out to the lanai and sat in her lounge chair. "I can fly, my son, my son." My father, Ray, had often said "my son, my son," and Mom adopted it as needed, as praise or criticism. She smiled brilliantly with her upper dentures held in place with only two solid teeth, receding gums that survived the Depression and 60 years beyond. She still had a firm demeanor, a certain and powerful presence, and laughed with great joy in her defiance. "You're my goddamned son," she joked and smiled, looking at me like her mother must've looked at her. "And I'm still the driver of the car," she said. "Remember, I've still got a license to drive."

I laughed. "I know you can fly. I remember how you drove that Impala in Fairfax." I sat beside her on a simple, white metal chair and didn't want to fight with her. Her driver's license had expired shortly after her recent accident. "What you told me about getting away from the farm, way back when, was remarkable, Mom. But please...."

"Yeah. I *can* fly!" she insisted. Her eyes gleamed as she stood and swung in a circle with her arms out as if wearing her favorite mink coat. I reached out to catch her, but she never fell, ever poised. Her prized garment shimmered as the invisible fur coat flew out around her like wings. It was as real and as elegant as the beating heart in her breast. "Dad," she said, "I joined the U.S. Army and I'm flying out on a big C-47 to Japan next month! We're planning to fly beyond Guam, Iwo Jima, and Wake Islands where the troops won battles in the war."

*Marj in her favorite mink coat.*

I had heard about her stories of the trip to Japan. She looked into the sky reflected on windows of her home, a double-wide trailer that she traded down from a fine Victorian five years earlier. She was pragmatic and tough, and her money grew and grew. Now she was confused about the passage of time, and as her illness became more apparent, I would sell her trailer for pennies on the dollar months later, when I moved her into the rest home. With her reluctant agreement.

"Mom, I'm your son, not your father."

"Yes, yes, yes. Michael. Of course."

Her father, Michael Fassler, was a bassoon player in the Sacramento Philharmonic. I was named for him. He was famous for occasionally driving to Lee Vining, a lawless town on the east side of the Sierra Nevada Mountains, with bootlegged whiskey in the days of Prohibition. And he was famous for being drunk. While delivering the hooch, he played gigs outside of Bridgeport with his friends. How he managed to drive over that treacherous pass, drunk and singing, I was told, back to the Central Valley, was anybody's guess. His paid job with the federal government was to shake one-half of Sacramento County's agricultural bounty of fruit—apricots, peaches, apples, and pears—off the trees to rot on the ground so that the rest would sell for a higher price in L.A., Stockton, and Sacramento. At night, he went back and gathered the forbidden fruit and distributed it to his friends and family, who had almost nothing during the hard times in the 1940s. That was his contribution to our family: a bit of compassion. That compassion was tempered with his raging drunken binges, and Mom never told me how they affected her spirit. But perhaps they were part of the reason she had taken flight to San Francisco.

"Well, I got to Japan, didn't I?" Mom looked at me with anger and continued speaking, seeming to continue proving her worth to her father. "I brought back three full 'short snorters' of signatures from my new friends and three good-luck ivory carvings." Short snorters were the prize of air travelers when they made a transoceanic voyage in the 1940s; all the passengers, pilots, and crew members on a flight signed their names on silver certificate one-dollar bills, proving their membership in this exclusive club of travelers. She had trained as a medical technician before going overseas, and she spent two years in Tokyo staining slides and looking at them in a microscope to help define diseases other service people may have caught. She loved that job because of what she learned in the lab and because of the people she had met there: journalists covering post-war times and the intrigue of many nationalities that came during the rebuilding of Japan.

Now she looked out toward the foothills of Boise for a moment as she laughed at some memory of Japan. "We flew to Hawaii, Guam, and the Philippines, but coming home was the most glorious scene. Back to the USA! Back to California! We got drunk just like you did." She held more secrets in her jade-green eyes. "I wish you had seen the beauty of that rich blue sky as we flew to Japan. We were held up in nothing but air, nothing but thin air, Dad, as we moved so quickly forward."

"In those days, it was thrilling to fly to a foreign country, and Japan was as exotic as the dark side of the moon!" She looked at me intensely to underscore the oddity of going to the Far East and shook her head. "The turquoise ocean around the South Sea Islands, with rings of coral around them—oh, you should see them, Dad! You can't imagine. It was so beautiful! The big island of Honshu stretched out before us. Then we landed right there in Tokyo. I absolutely loved Tokyo, but things were not so good there." She looked at the clear Idaho sky, but I imagined the devastation from the atomic bomb blasts in Japan. "After work at the lab, I went walking to tea houses and tasted dozens of kinds of teas—Oolong, Ceylon, Darjeeling, and lots of others. it was illegal to serve those Chinese teas." She paused and shook her head. "Mt. Fuji looked so big. It stood out just like California's Mt. Shasta."

She went on like that, reciting memories, as I listened to her. "Cherry blossoms filled the sky with flying petals that fell and paved roads with setting suns. It was beautiful!" She shook her head. "I saw the dying cultures of geisha and the samurai whose time in the sun was killed by the dropping of the atomic bomb. That's all gone now. All of it." She shook her head again and looked down and spoke slowly. "But I've always thought that the flowers will remain like suns on the streets of Tokyo every spring. It was gorgeous. I was blessed to have seen all of that in my life."

"Do you want some water, Mom?"

"Yeah, umm, yes, water." Her eyes had a thin film over them. "Where is Ray?" She was still confused in time. Time moved quickly, now. The chronology of moments, however, failed miserably, mattering so little as we sat side-by-side, as she reminisced about her past.

"Mom, Dad died 45 years ago. You remember, he died of brain cancer and a stroke?"

"Oh yes, I remember that. It was malignant, wasn't it?" She thought for a moment. "I always thought it was from the radiation. He was an observer in Nevada, you know." She looked down for a moment. "Well. He was a wonderful man in many ways, wasn't he? Such a good man! He bought blueberry muffins for me at Blum's in San Francisco. They were the best things I've ever eaten!" Her eyes softened, but then her wrinkles deepened. "He did have his problems, didn't he?" She paused. "Is he at home?"

"I don't know, Mom. Maybe."

△△△

Where do the dead go when they go home? Into oblivion, flying high into the wild blue yonder? Into memories of songs and movies? Into the minds of those who knew them when they were alive? This is curious to me. What would happen to all of us? Perhaps we have a half-life after dying, like the life of radioactive isotopes that give up half of their power with every passing generation. Or do our faces simply fade over the years? Like the reflecting images in an aging tintype? I have a tintype photo of my great, great, grandmother—she looks so stern—and I was told of her husband's ice-making business. I was given his 1880s National Watch Company pocket watch that still keeps perfect railroad time, even in 2021. I keep it with me.

I met my grandfather and have seen his carvings made of dinosaur bones from a trip to Alaska, his finely hewed end tables—and I hear his scratchy voice. I own his superbly carpentered mahogany quarter-cabinet, which sits boldly in my living room. These things I revere, along with my father's pure white Meerschaum pipe with the bearded Turkish head upon it, his Seiko watch that runs when it is shaken, the small solar panel from 1963 that was headed to one of the first satellites that was shot into space, but for a defect. I have Mom's signed print of Salvador Dali's black stallion, her lucky ivory carvings, and a Marc Chagall print of a man overlooking a breasty female artist. By these things I divine what remains important to my family's mix of values, and what is left behind for me to enjoy. They define me.

But what do I have of my own? Fading memories? The houses I've built, pictures that I've taken, lucky stones that I've gathered, memories of women I've loved, places I've helped protect, Mom's good-luck ivory carvings, and all of my writing? Is all of that nothing? I don't know. Still, I breathe. Still remember. Still walk and run. Still love.

Already, in late midlife, this is a fading legacy: they are things seen in a rearview mirror. No kids. No siblings. No wife. Ah, but I am bejeweled with rubies, emeralds, and diamond-dust from Jaipur, hunks of jade from the Kobuk River in Alaska, flat skipping stones from the Colville River in the Arctic, conch shells found along the Delaware shore, a shark tooth from a dry mountain in Utah, memories of porpoises breaking waves in Oahu, the image of fishermen standing on a jetty in Delaware, the rattlesnake in a canyon in southern Utah, the glowing red tide late at night on a beach in Central California. And all of my friends. There is, indeed, magic in this world! And in the memories of it.

I tell stories of my mom in her prime and beyond, that now seem somehow wonderful and true to me, but they are warped significantly by my memories of them. What experiences have I had? Ha! I survived a stroke. But that is past and mostly forgotten. I have stories to tell, but what will my children know of me? Nothing! I have no children. I would simply prefer to live forever. I want to be amazing. Live in the dream-world of Emperor Norton. And not die in a crumpled mass of broken memories, regrets, and weaknesses. Maybe there will be more time to correct my kinked-up life. But I am so small.

△△△

"You don't know, my son!"

"Well let's forget about that, Mom," I yelled.

"Oh no, no, no, we won't forget about him."

"Ray was your husband for 13 years, Mom, of course you'll remember."

"Oh yes, it's been more than 13 years; it's been 62 years now." She stopped and looked at the ceiling. "I was almost 30 when I met him in Long Island after the war. He was the most debonair man! A lieutenant colonel and then a full colonel, but a lawyer by trade. With a pistol in his hand, because he was an actor, he told me." She laughed and spoke remarkably clearly. "That was plain silly. But he had a Chris-Craft and that was a *very sexy boat*! Very sexy. It sunk one night in a nasty storm." She paused and smiled as she ran through her memories. "Before that, he took me out in his boat and we roamed on Long Island Sound." Now she looked unblinkingly at me and told me her story.

"Mike, we were so romantic back in those days. That was the first place he asked me to marry him!" Her eyes always held youth when she talked about Ray. They opened and blinked coquettishly as she traveled back decades to times of her youth. "That bum lived, but the boat was never the same." She chuckled. "It got broken up in that wicked storm in Long Beach." She put a hand over her mouth to keep from laughing out loud. "The tie-offs on the pier led straight down to the sunken boat. Oh, it was so sad when we got up in the morning and looked out the window at the motorboat. It was so, so sad. All we saw at first was the dock. And then we saw what had happened. I just laughed and Ray was so furious!" She was silent for a moment. "But the oysters we shared the night before at the Oyster Bar in Grand Central were fabulous. There must've been 20 kinds of oysters, Asharokens from Long Island and Blue Diamonds from

Washington State. I ended up walking home alone all through the night. We were just crazy. God, were we crazy." She looked at me as if I would never understand what passion was. Her head bobbed, her lips tightened, her eyes closed as she looked at mirages of her past.

△△△

Marj and Ray after a swim in the Bahamas.

"Marj, will you marry me?" Ray proposed to her, not on his knees, not with a diamond in his hands, but with her hand in his and his face at her level.

"Sure. I would love to!" She slurped the last oyster with slick garlic-butter and it slid quickly down her throat. She kissed him slowly and pushed him away. "But Ray, there is something I haven't told you."

"What's that?"

"Like you, I'm legally married."

"You're what?" Ray's face turned bright red in a second.

"I'm married to Jim Norton."

"To Jim? You've got to be kidding!" Ray's napkin fell to the floor. "Why didn't you tell me? What are you doing here, Marj?"

"I didn't think that we would move along so quickly." She wiped a smudge from her lips and noticed the rough red smudges on Ray's mouth. "I'm having the marriage annulled. It is you whom I love, Colonel Medberry."

"An-nulled." He lit a cigarette slowly and his butane lighter flamed like a blow torch. "So you weren't *ac-tual-ly* married?"

"Well, no, I mean we are married. But no priest held the service. It's embarrassing, Ray. We just, we just didn't get along." She picked up the napkin and touched it to the corners of her mouth then handed it to Ray with a look that suggested he clean up a bit. "Excuse me." She stood and walked, with the practiced clickity-clack of her high heels on a path toward the ladies' room.

Ray watched the seam of her nylons as she walked away and smoked his cigarette to the nub. She came back quite composed, with crimson lipstick brilliant against her pale skin, looking as flawless as Hedy Lamarr. "Can you accept that? We just didn't get along." She stood over Ray and he stood up to face her. She snapped open her clutch at his face level, looked into it, and found her mad money. She closed it as loudly and dramatically as she could and awaited his response.

"Well I don't know." He sat back down, sensing his power, and lit a second cigarette, while the first smoked in the ashtray. He blew a smoke ring that wobbled into air. "What happened?"

"Nothing. Let's just leave it there."

"OK. In that case, this dinner is finished. Let me pay the bill and we can go if you'd like. Or we can go have a drink and talk about it."

She heard only that he still wanted to have a drink with her. "Have you got your divorce from old what's-her-name finalized?"

"No, no, it's been a little tough to get the divorce...."

"I'll bet." She looked straight at him. Her lips tightened.

"Marj...." He stood up again.

"It seems that we've both got some work to do." Marj turned her back on Ray, and then stopped, turned to look at him. "I'll get a taxi and a motel room. I'll see you next week. And, Ray, I accept your damned proposal."

"Marj, hold on! That's wonderful! Let's at least finish dinner." He spoke too loudly.

"Dinner can wait until we're both divorced." She spoke softly toward the tables of other people around them. "Now, don't follow me" she said, hinting at what she might have wanted him to do. She turned and walked out of the restaurant, the sharp staccato of her high heels making echoes in the diner, forcing other customers to become her audience. When she was gone a few diners glanced surreptitiously at Ray.

"At ease," he said to the nosy people. "God damn it," he muttered, smashing his cigarette into the ashtray. Dramatically, he paid the bill and walked out of the restaurant, stoic as a soldier walking out of war. He fully intended to follow Marj.

△△△

Now, as I walked slowly toward the rest home, I dreaded what I might find when I arrived. My mind continued to wander. Mom had told me about her older brother, Jack, when we lived near him in Sacramento, after my dad died when I was 12. I stared at a small fountain in my neighbor's garden that was covered with ice. Mom moved the two of us from the well-appointed home she and my father had lived in in Hancock Park, Los Angeles, when the memories of his death slipped around in that old house like ghosts. She carried us north, nearer to her mother's small home in Sacramento, and we arrived just a block away from the American River, in a place that still reminds me of something out of Mark Twain's *Tom Sawyer*. There was still innocence to corrupt along that river: a fishing pole hung beside our back door, a raft was nearby to launch, and three friends and I had time to kill every summer.

My favorite fishing spot was in a gravel pit beside the river in Sacramento. There were lakes on one side and a dirt road with the river beside it. We had conjured up some character at the liquor store to buy beer for us, and after my high school friends, Doug Rathkamp and Dave Marten, and I got to the "pits," we—all of us—soon were fighting a 5- or 6-pound shad at the same moment. That happened more frequently than you might expect, with the fish running together in packs from the ocean. One of us would yell, "Pandemonium!" And the other would shout, "Fuckin'-A, Fish On!" This was the manly thing to do: drink Lucky Lager beer with puzzles on the inside of the bottle caps, catch big-assed fish, and scream out words for the sake of their sound, feeling as if we were corrupting the whole damned, fucking world.

I thought about the fish I loved. Shad are thin but as broadsided as a scimitar blade. They provide a scrappy fight when they turn downstream and swim cross-current. When a hooked shad fights on the surface of the water, its scales shine like quarter-sized sequins, and when it jumps, it soars high and mighty, flashing its tail, leaping for the sun! Shad, however, are bony and tougher than carp, meaner than steelhead, quicker than salmon, and smarter than sturgeon, but not very tasty, and so, generally, they earned their release. I gave thanks when I released each one and returned to my illicit beer and read the newest riddle on the Lucky Lager bottle cap. It was always pretty stupid when you figured it out. I sang the jingle and offered a toast: "It's Lu-ckey when you live out West; the West is Lu-ckey country!" It was sort of a duffus song, but we all sang badly and loud and got silly.

One night, however, after I wobbled home from an evening of lively shad fishing and trolling for beer, Mom told me about something that happened in her youth in the 1930s in Sacramento. I'd handed her the shad, and I guess the story was on her mind as she painted ink on the big fish and rolled it across some art paper. I was aghast that she put all of that black ink on my gorgeous fish, because it was a keeper, a big fish; it seemed fat enough to bake and would provide lots of roe. However, she wasn't in a baking mood, and today that inky image of the shad hangs on my kitchen wall.

But I began telling you about Jack, Mom's big brother, not really about my life as a kid, and this story was one that Mom told me when we had walked down along the American River in the early '70s, in the glory days of shad fishing:

"Kids," Mom said, quoting her mother. "You kids have to stay at home tonight while your dad is playing music at the Cliff House, down at the ocean."

"Mom, can't we just come and listen?" Jack said. He was nearly 6 feet tall and 19 years old, but still he bitched endlessly and therefore still qualified as a kid. He looked a little like Red Skelton. Come to think of it, it was Jack who I pictured when I heard Red Skelton joking on the radio many years ago. Jack was jovial like that and kind of funny looking as well, with a big red nose. He was the life of the party and often inappropriately so.

"No, of course not. Jack, would you mind taking charge of the kids for this evening while we're gone?" She asked the question, but really, it was a demand.

"No. Sure I would, Mom," Jack whined. He smiled almost maniacally. "I'll watch 'em climbing in and out of the windows! One of 'em'll break a neck sure as I'm Michael Fassler's kid. That is, if I am...."

"Goddammit Jack, I mean it! Don't be fresh with your mother or I'm going to smack you to the floor! Your father is playing at Cliff House and this could be a big break for him."

"Yes, of course, I'll stay and watch the kids." Jack sounded demure, but he was still full of himself just the same, like the older brother he was. He pulled his sister Marjie aside. His breath smelled of baloney. "Marjie, let's go to the Sutro Baths, you know, maybe sneak in and go to the big Cliff House up the hill from there. They have fancy, heated swimming pools at Sutros. We can go if you want." He pinched Marjie hard on her butt, or that's what my mom told me anyway. "Just to see what's brewing there and listen to Dad playing the clarinet and sax."

A postcard from Sutro Baths in the 1930s.

"No more pinching, Jackass!" She hit Jack hard on his shoulder and then beamed and offered him a conspiratorial smile. "OK, Jack," she said to the side. "Let's do it and sneak in. The kids are old enough to take care of themselves, right?"

"Yeah, maybe. We can lock all of the doors and tell them to go to sleep. Herb'll watch 'em."

That afternoon, Jack and Marjie took the streetcar downtown and then to Sutro Baths, a bit north of the Cliff House, on a special trolley that left on the hour from the city. The ride was crowded and they got out beside Sutro's, Mom told me, with a crew of drunken sailors.

She held her brother by his shoulders and whispered into an ear. "Hey Jack, pretend to be a valet, get a couple bucks from the drivers, and then let's go in the front door." They had stopped beside a parking lot.

"Why don't you?"

"No, you're the big joker!"

"Alright, alright. But you figure how to get into the Cliff House to hear Dad. You've got the looks, Marjie. And I've got the brains. Deal?"

"Yeah, deal." She smiled. "But I think you've got that backward, Jackal. You've got a big head, and mine, well, it's a bit smaller and much prettier." She primped her locks. "You know what they say about that?" She wasn't about to give Jack the chance to respond. "Big head full of shit; little head full of wit!" She smacked him on the back.

"You little shit." He left it at that. "I'll bet Dad knocks 'em dead! Just wait and see. Unless he gets to drinking."

Mom said that Jack talked his way into the first car that came in to be parked in the lot, sweet-talked a driver out of the second, and parked both cars blocking the exit. He found a sawbuck in one of the glove boxes and slipped it into his pocket. "Okay, little sister," he said, swaggering up to her as he handed the stolen bill to her.

They opened the massive oak door to Sutro Baths that was decorated with scrimshaw designs of whales and mermaids, and walked up the wide, spiraling staircase to visit what was pitched as the "Grand, Phenomenal, New West Museum." I've seen the photos of stuffed lions, tigers, a narwhal, and a walrus with its deadly tusks. They had seen none of these wild animals and admitted none of their wide-eyed admiration for them. Their admiration, however, fell on the mummies, the honest-to-God Egyptian mummies, the thousands-of-years-old dead people from a far-away, parched land. Afterward, Jack and Marjie stood above the faux Hawaiian beach with real palm trees, umbrellas, and white sand beside one of those Olympic-sized saltwater swimming pools.

"Pinch me. You think that beach is real?" she said.

"Yeah, it's real. Real hokey, is what I think. But I won't pinch you. I've learned."

"Good boy!" She smiled crookedly. "Let's go down there. Let's swim in Hawaii."

"And see the Grand, Phenomenal, Panorama of the Western World?"

"Yeah, I think so."

They sauntered down to the entrance and traded ten dollars for a bathing suit and swimming trunks, and received in return a fat chunk of change, which Jack stuffed into his pants pockets. They changed clothes into bathing suits in two booths and slipped down a pole to splash into refreshing saltwater.

"Hooo-we! Jack, this is great!"

"Sure is! We should have done this way before now." They got out after half an hour, satisfied and wrinkled.

"Okay, Marjie," Jack said, putting his wrinkled feet into his shoes. "Now you get us into the Cliff House, and remember, let's not be seen by our parents."

"Alright, follow me just like you like me, Jackie boy."

"Whatever you say, sis."

When they got to the door of the Cliff House, Jack handed the doorman a five-dollar bill, and they found seats that weren't visible to their parents. They heard lots of laughing and clicking of glasses and then silence, when the announcer emerged on the stage, facing the microphone.

"Ladies and gentlemen, I would like to introduce one of San Francisco's upcoming jazz artists, Michael Fassler. Michael has played in the Sacramento Symphony and has played in a quartet down in Galt. He claims to deliver moonshine to the boys in Bridgeport, but I wouldn't say that's for sure. Please lend him a hearty hand!"

But Michael never got up to play, because he was passed-out, his head resting on the mahogany bar. Mom told me that she and Jack sneaked out and walked home to their place on Sutter Street. They left the surging surf beside Cliff House, flew through the wild sounds and smells of Chinatown, with the neon lights burning on this warm San Francisco night, in silence.

△△△

Mom told me about the Sutro Baths on one of nearly half-a-dozen trips we took to the Curran Theatre in San Francisco when I was in college. She told me what occurred with her once-upon-a-time, almost-husband, Jim Norton, while she was in Japan. She had gone to a restaurant when both of them were in the States, and there she nullified the marriage. Before that, however, Jim and Marj had fun and bickered like two siblings.

For example, Jim had arranged for a photo shoot with Mom the year after she arrived in Japan, when she was an airman first class and he was a captain. "Marj, how about you get up on the wing of the DC 4. It's only...."

"You think I'm going to climb up there just for you to take a goddamned picture of me in my tight dress? Jimmie baby, honey, you've got another fat thing comin'. And it'll taste like cheap, rock-

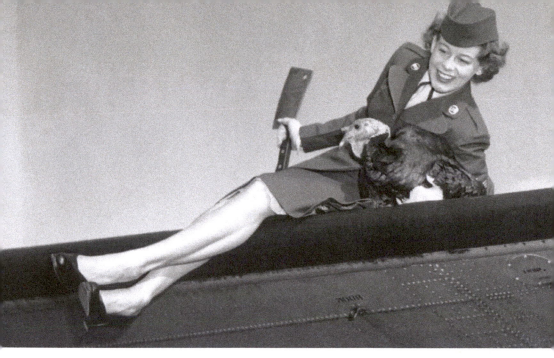

Marj on the wing of a plane in the 1940s.

gut whiskey." That's what she told me she said, but you know how conversations become inflated with the passage of time. But the picture that I saw of her years later led me to believe she'd told me the truth.

Jim laughed. "It would be a good shot with you on the wing, you've got to admit! "Okay, you climb up and I'll stand down here. That way, we'll get an interesting perspective. I think it would be better if you were out there on the wing."

"Yeah, right. So exactly what am I going to do out there on the wing? Eat turkey?"

"Well, let me think." He looked directly at her face. "You left Galt, but you used to work with chickens, right?"

"Only if my mother was there forcing me to get the eggs! And she, I will remind you, Jim, is not here."

"Okay, how about a Thanksgiving theme? I like your turkey idea."

"Yeah, and you want me to wield a hatchet to cut its throat?"

Jim laughed. "Ho, ho, ho, that's a great idea, Marj! But don't struggle with it. I mean the turkey. That could get messy." Jim turned to a flyboy film assistant. "Sergeant, can you find a turkey?"

"Very funny, Jim," Marj interrupted. "Why don't we try something else?"

"Yeah, Jim," the flyboy said. "We've got a bunch of turkeys that were flown in from the States for Thanksgiving. Great idea!"

"Oh no. Guys, please. I don't want to go up there with a shitting turkey struggling with me trying to balance and me with my high heels and the uniform that will get filthy, no way guys. No lousy way!"

"It would be a great shot!" Jim insisted. He grinned. "People would look at you with a turkey and a hatchet and everyone would laugh. That would be hilarious. The press would use it and the brass would be very amused."

"Oh, great," Marj said.

"It's a memorable shot. And Marj, with those legs...."

"Knock it off, Jimbo."

"OK, OK, we could do something else...."

"No, alright, let's do it for the brass, but you have to help me climb up and get on the wing. And I don't want to slip down so you're going to have to back me up. And you can't move the ladder like you did in that last photo shoot!" Marj laughed at him, but she teased Jim as he moved a ladder to her. She thought about dropping an egg on his head. But alas, no eggs to drop. Her mother wasn't there to criticize her, and Jim, in any case, would be thrilled.

"I promise," he snickered. "I'd be happy to help you get up and down from the wing. Just don't let your hat blow off. Hold the hat, alright?"

"That would be so *déclassé*," she teased, "to lose my hat, you dirty bastard!"

*Marj wearing her
alpaca coat.*

△△△

After I left for college, Mom moved to L.A. and then back to the gold country of Jackson, California, oddly, or appropriately, to the very town where Jim Norton lived. Come to think of it, maybe my mom lived a more unconventional life than I had. Jim had gotten married and Marj was widowed, and it never occurred to me to think about what they had done in Japan, or what either of them did to each other's soul. I was as ignorant as the day is of impending night. Which is to say, I might just figure it out if I was patient.

"Hey Jim," Marj said at a dinner for five that I was invited to. "I've always wanted to fly." This was news to me. She left it there and let the comment find home.

"Oh?" Jim picked up his knife and smiled at Marj. His reaction was odd enough to get my attention. Jim's daughter was a knockout, but she was planning to go to a concert that night and was not yet dolled-up. She excused herself and my eyes followed her out as I gobbled the last piece of steak on my plate. "Have you?" Jim said, with an odd cock of his head. He had landed a job as a flight teacher after his 15-year military career.

"Yes," Marj said brightly. "I loved to see the world from above. And now I want to choose my own path."

"I thought you'd always done that?" Jim said with a stone-cold look, setting his knife down. Jim, I now see in retrospect, had a dry and understated sense of humor. He did not miss Marj's naïve-seeming subtlety. Mom chuckled and almost choked on her food. She was never one to miss an opportunity for commentary, sarcasm, or double entendre. Neither, apparently, was Jim.

"Only when it came my way," she said. "I just wanted to engage you as a flight teacher to show me the ropes."

"Alright," he said taking the bait—but, I thought, doubting that she would actually show up. Sometimes we never learn. "Be on the tarmac at 8 a.m. Saturday and we'll begin the process." Mary, Jim's wife, stood up and cleared the plates, making one hell of a racket.

Jim taught Marj to fly in a small Cessna, and she took it on like her first Chevrolet Impala, with gusto. She went up four or five times, and on her first solo flight she got lost between Sutter Creek and Galt. She wound up in Porterville, being lectured by the staff at two control towers, demanding that she get the plane out of the way of direct continental flights. She landed in Porterville with the help of commentary from a controller, who guided her gently to the ground. She called Jim and explained her circumstances, and Jim drove down and flew her plane back north to the little tarmac near Sutter Creek. "The sky is more crowded than it was in the '40s," Jim said. She agreed, and never got in another plane alone. Jim, however, always seemed amused by Marj, much to the dander of his long-suffering wife.

△△△

I took a deep breath and thought about what I might see inside the doors of the rest home. Mom had signed a card that she carried in her wallet for 22 years on which was written the following: "If there is no reasonable expectation of my recovery in my extreme physical or mental disability, I direct that I be allowed to die.... I hope that you who care for me will feel morally bound to act in accordance with this urgent request." She had chosen not to take the prescribed thyroid medication she had needed. The endocrinologist didn't approve of Mom refusing the thyroxin; he knew the misery that was in store for her.

Mom had walked like an Olympic champion for most of the last 60 years when I knew her, but in her final years, she didn't get outside at all because her dog wouldn't budge. She loved her dog, Tank, who wholly fit his name. She fed him everything he wanted, so, eventually, he died from overeating. No kidding, overeating. She survived breast cancer three years before, but it took a toll on her body. She slowed down on this flying glide to the ground without thyroxin and she hurt in every imaginable way as her metabolism shut down. A pharmacist told me that not taking thyroxin might be a peaceful way to die. However, that was not the case for her.

I recalled a discussion that I had with a hospice nurse two days before:

"Morphine, morphine, MORE MORPHINE!" I insisted.

"We can't do that. We can't give her morphine unless she is suffering."

"She *is* suffering." I whispered viciously and looked through her face. "That hole in her back is exploding like the atomic bomb!" Mom's latest problem was a deadly Kennedy terminal ulcer, an unhealing wound that develops rapidly during the final states of a person's death, as organs catastrophically fail. I believed this was happening because of her failure to take the thyroxin medication. And it spoke of the unhealed part of her that would never be erased—for better or worse, she had chosen this way to die, and I was her accomplice.

"You'll kill her," she said.

"That is the fucking idea. She is in a world of hurt! She is now 91 and that's a pretty damned long life."

"I can't do that."

"You said you would increase her dose if she is suffering. She is. They did it for the soldiers who were shot during the Civil War and World War I and World War II."

"That was a different time, in different circumstances. She'll go the way of God."

"Which way is that? She has never believed in God."

"Yes, she has."

"Nurse, let's not argue; please just give her some morphine."

"I can't do that. This is Idaho. It is not legal."

"I thought you were a nurse, dedicated, first, to compassion."

"I am."

"Then goddamn well prove it!" I stormed out of the room.

△△△

A morning beam of sunlight cut through the dark sky of brooding rainclouds with a blinding silvery incandescence as I walked through a park toward the rest home. I won't say it was a beautiful sight, nor was it some gift from God, but it was unusual, an eerie sight, a bewitching one. I stopped and watched a dove calling out from bare trees in the park. Its coos sounded lonely and elegant, coming from nothing and for no apparent reason. It was just a dove, but the timing fit the contour of my soul, and the bird sat and called out again and again. This simple song of nature brought joy to me, as nature always has, and I felt responsibility for my mother, who ever-so-gently flew from solid, to lighter, to ethereal, and ultimately to the floating lightness of death. And, I hoped, to endless peace and love. I understood that my life would end at some time in a circumstance perhaps much like hers, and in the meantime, I should live exactly as I wanted to, exactly as I deserved, exactly as if I had come here to fly into this light on a cold, misty day and walk no more.

When I entered her darkened room, Mom was stretching her arms up to the sky, with her eyes closed. It was not yet her time. Not yet. But soon. I sat beside her and opened her book, the *Rubaiyat of Omar Khayyam*, intending to read a few of her favorite rhymes to her. But she was not present. She reached for the God she had forgotten and left for dead. I felt surprised to see this occult presence in her, and watched her reckoning on the path from here to immortality. As life always must be at the end.

As the light dimmed in the late night, she reached for this new awareness, sleepwalking in her bedroom, dreaming, with nightmares, in the presence of a God she never told me she knew. She struggled and would not go with him. No, he hadn't made a believer of her. He had never stepped in to avoid her rape. Was that villain her father, or a sailor with a hook on his arm like some Blackbeard, or an unknown stranger? I would never know. But God seemed familiar enough, and kindly. She reached up and withdrew her arms and reached again in the dark to offer her compliance, her forgiveness, her acceptance to this spirit of everlasting love. Such a view of torture on one side, I now realized, is the view of bliss on the other: the beauty of a life lived fully, forgiving, and given up. It was hard to forgive, it was a life's work, and now she didn't want to go. She had done all of the hard work. But all too soon, her heart stopped pumping and her mind flew away.

△△△

*The urn from which Mom's ashes emerged.*

After she died, I put Mom's ashes in three places: in the Pacific Ocean below the ruins of the Sutro Baths, beside my father's resting place in Los Angeles, and in the yard of my new home—all places that are memorable for me. I don't know what they would have meant to my mom.

I walked along the ocean by the burned and wrecked monument of the Sutro Baths, with my girlfriend, Roxanne, and my longtime friend, Dave Martin, carrying Mom's ashes in a porcelain urn with butterflies painted on it. We walked into a modest surf before the shore and then into the waves and I set the urn in the sand. When the ashes washed out from the urn, they bubbled and sighed and burst in a line toward San Francisco Bay, as if the bay, and perhaps the wild blue yonder, was, at long last, hers, as the butterflies took flight.

# FOOTBALL PLAYING IN BOISE, IDAHO

A boy lies in the Saint Luke's Hospital recovery unit. Coach Pete sits beside him. "Can you lift your hand, son?" Pete asks. He's been told that he can at least do that. Pete has come to the boy's side at a request of the boy's parents in the hope that he will provide some inspiration.

"Not so much." He smiles. A hose comes out of his nose and a thin cord slips into his arm. He's wearing a helmet of gauze. His hand just lies there on his lap.

Coach Pete says nothing but returns the smile.

"Let me try again." He struggles with that gut strength that comes out of nowhere. His hand rises to grip a cup. His finger curls instinctively to hold onto it.

"That's good!" Pete says. He can see that the boy is a damn hard fighter. That's what he's been told. It's what he sees. He sees that the boy may be back in time for the last game.

"You think?" You can tell the boy doesn't think so. He is so lost without full use of his limbs.

"Yes, I know." He does know. The coach has seen many miracles before. "You have to want a thing very much or it will never be." Pete's smile costs nothing to look at; it gives the boy a million bucks.

The boy closes his eyes and sees himself out on the field running as a football floats out of the sky into his outstretched hands. It is in his smile forevermore.

# ACKNOWLEDGEMENTS

I would like to thank Toni Rome for her work at designing and giving me advice on this book. And I offer my gratitude to Colleen Brennan, Steve Bunk, Lisa Theobald, John McCarthy, Rich Rayhill, Jima Rice, and Doug Schnitzspahn for good advice, editing, and help at publishing; Thank you to Scott Gipson for his generous support and kindness in dealing with my writing. To Char Roth, I'm grateful for walking along Arch Canyon Creek many years ago and for friendship between there and here. For Sue Randall, I offer profound friendship; she lived through my sunrise to sunset Solstice walks which, occasionally lasted a wee-bit longer than planned. Thank you to all of my writing group members from the superb Community of Writers Workshops in Olympic Valley near Lake Tahoe and for all of the slightly loony Zoom discussions as we avoided the most recent pandemic. To Roxanne Ybarguen, who was kind and loving to my mother and me in a time full of sorrow, I remain grateful.

I'm also offering thanks to Native American Tribes who originally lived on the land which I have hiked upon. Those tribes include Shoshone-Bannock (Newe), Kootenai (Ktunxa), Coeur d'Alene (Shitsu'umish), Shoshone-Paiute (Newe-Numa), Nez Perce (Nimipuu), Goshute, Tongva, Gabrielneo, "Anasazi," Navajo, Hopi, Ute, Zuni, and Inupiat (Eskimo) people. I am grateful to federal bureaucracies for preserving nature and wild places to walk, including the U.S. Forest Service, Bureau of Land Management, the Fish and Wildlife Service, the National Park Service, National Wildlife Refuges, and others. They have assured that significant parts of our land and vast numbers of wildlife remain managed for and by the public, as indecisive and combative as we sometimes are.

Having said all of that, I recognize that no one can own or manages any piece of land for long. That may be the greatest gift of all as we are always changing and learning to see things differently. Mine is but a snapshot in time and I hope that humanity comes to recognize that we have the whole world in our hands in coming days. The world is a very fragile, precious place to live. We can hold it with love. If we choose to do so.

**M**ike Medberry has written essays on conservation and place-based issues in the West for *Mountain Gazette*, *Idaho Magazine*, *Limberlost Press*, *Sierra*, *High Country News*, *The Blue Review*, *The Mountain Express*, *Northern Lights*, *Stroke Connection*, *The Boise Weekly*, among others, and for the books *Idaho Wilderness Considered* and *River by Design*. He has published short stories, was an Artist in Residence for the city of Boise, has taught classes on writing the memoir, has edited several published books, and authored the book *On the Dark Side of the Moon*, about surviving a severe stroke. He was a lead staff person for the Wilderness Society, Idaho Conservation League, Hells Canyon Preservation Council, and other organizations for three decades. He has an M.F.A. from the University of Washington.

△△△

Several of these essays were originally published in slightly different form in the following:

▷ "The Art and War of Wilderness" in *The Blue Review and The Boise Weekly*

▷ "A Day in the Slammer" in *The Star News*

▷ "Dark Side of the Moon" in *On the Dark Side of the Moon* and *The Writer's Workshop*

▷ "Eluding Antarctica" in *Mountain Gazette*

▷ "French Creek: Lost in a Lost Drainage" in *Idaho Magazine*

▷ "In the Land of the Midnight Sun" in the electronic and shorter version in *Sierra* magazine

▷ "Of Science and Sanity" in *Idaho Magazine*

▷ "Walking Up the Boise River" in *Idaho Magazine* and *Idaho Wilderness Considered*

▷ "Walking the L.A. River" in *The Blue Review*, *Limberlost Press*, and *Mountain Gazette*

In addition, the shorter essays, "Football Playing in Boise," "Two Dead Deer," "A Fool's Drunken Pilgrimage in Search of a Gila Monster" (under the previous title "The Gila Monster Arrives"), "Home," "A Day in the Slammer," and "A Cat's Story," can be found on my WordPress website: mikemedberry.com

CPSIA information can be obtained
at www.ICGtesting.com
Printed in the USA
LVHW071617050422
715394LV00008B/431